BATTLEZONE

D1373973

BATTLEZONE

ARMING YOURSELF TO
WAGE WAR WITH THE DEVIL

GREG STIER

MOODY
PUBLISHERS

CHICAGO

© 2003 by
GREG STIER

All Scripture quotations, unless otherwise marked, are taken from
the *Holy Bible, New International Version*®. NIV®. Copyright ©
1973, 1978, 1984 by International Bible Society. Used by permission
of Zondervan Publishing House. All rights reserved.

Scripture quotations marked KJV are taken from the King James
Version.

Book Design: *www.DesignByJulia.com*

Library of Congress Cataloging-in-Publication Data
Stier, Greg.
    Battle zone : arming yourself to wage war with the Devil /
    Greg Stier.
    p. cm.
    ISBN 0-8024-1793-0
    1. Spiritual warfare. I. Title.

BV4509.5.S845 2003
235′.4--dc21
                                    2003009486

1   3   5   7   9   10   8   6   4   2
Printed in the United States of America

To the thousands of
young warriors
who I have had the privilege
of training
at Dare2Share conferences
over the years.

CONTENTS

FOREWORD

I was there. It was not a battlefield that most would expect, perhaps the most unlikely place for a war to occur, yet the most real and evident example of modern day spiritual warfare. A small library tucked inside a typical suburban school called Columbine, the high school now famous for the most terrifying school shooting in United States history. I remember it clearly . . . a battle against innocent students, where lives were ended, our sense of security stripped away, and the lives of countless families changed forever.

As a junior in high school I entered the library that day not knowing it could be the last day of my life. When the two boys entered the room with the intent to kill using their guns and bombs, I clung to two other friends, praying, waiting to die. I will never forget when my friend told me that he would take a bullet for me. It was at that moment I vowed to serve the Lord with all my heart from then on. Up until then I wasn't living like a believer. In fact, up until that point I had tried everything to fill the void within my life. For several months I had been living a double life—as a Christian, but also as a person still craving the world. But that day changed everything. While I hid under a table in the Columbine library, a battle was raging around me and within me, a battle to choose once and for all who I would serve. I chose Jesus.

After seven minutes of sheer horror, the two boys who stood above our table were talking about leaving to reload their guns. It was when they left that we got up to escape and surveyed the damage of the room. Smoke filled the air, glass and books were thrown all over, and bodies were strewn everywhere. I was there, a survivor of tragedy and pain. Because I was there I can share with you a lesson I learned . . . the lesson of urgency.

We do not know what lies ahead, but we do know that God has a unique purpose for each of our lives. We also know that Satan wants to do whatever he can to distract us from Jesus. As young people, we constantly face this threat of spiritual warfare in this world. We must choose which kind of movies we will watch, the music we will listen to, and the life we will live. Satan's toys and temptations have the potential to tear us away from what really matters in life—knowing Christ and making Him known through word and action.

There is a great urgency for us as Christian teenagers to share the gospel with our lost friends and family so they too can experience the joy we have in our own lives. My prayer is that you will never have to encounter a situation like the one I did on April 20th, 1999, that forces you to choose whether or not you will surrender and follow after Christ with all your heart. I hope and pray that you choose Jesus now without something so catastrophic happening to you. May the world around you see the light within you, so they can experience victory in Jesus, who has already defeated the evil one through His blood shed for you and me. Do not let another second pass by without serving Him and sharing His message. There may not be another chance. Believe me, I know.

Crystal Woodman

BEFORE YOU BEGIN THIS JOURNEY

You are about to begin a wild and weird journey. It is a trip filled with evil creatures, angelic beings, and invisible battles that swirl around us all the time in the unseen world of the spiritual. It is a dangerous trip because it revolves around a war in the underworld for the soul of humanity. ✺

And the craziest part of the whole thing is this: You play a big part in this battle. You are a warrior, a soldier of the light in the army of God. He wants to use you to advance His cause, His kingdom, and His Christ. So Satan, the dark lord of the underworld, is unleashing the vast forces of powerful demons under his command to stop you in your tracks. The Evil One's goal is to keep you from living a life that counts for eternity. He wants to sidetrack you with sin, discourage you with trials, deceive you with lies, and distract you with toys, to use anything and everything at his disposal to make you an ineffective Christian witness. ✺

Yeah, I know, I know, it sounds like *Lord of the Rings* stuff of legend and make-believe. But it is very real. How do I know that? Because God's Word says it's real, and God doesn't play when it comes to telling the truth.

That's why I want to share a few principles with you before we begin this strange, wonderful, and dangerous journey into the subject of spiritual warfare. ✺

A BOOK YOU CAN TRUST

It's probably a good time to give you a quick crash course on why you can trust the Word of God when it comes to the basics of spiritual warfare (or any truth for that matter). Why? Because we are going to be talking about some pretty incredible stuff in the pages to follow. Some of the stories I'm going to share with you from God's Word will seem like the hocus-pocus myths of make-believe. But the Bible is not make-believe. It is deadly serious. Have you ever heard the phrase "Truth is stranger than fiction"? That really applies here. The truth of God's Word when it comes to spiritual warfare is much stranger than the best fiction of Lukas, Spielberg, Tolkien, or J. K. Rowling. ⚙

So here are a few reasons that you can trust God's Word when it makes seemingly unbelievable claims. ⓑ

GOD'S WORD CLAIMS TO BE TRUE

The Bible makes a bold proclamation in 2 Timothy 3:16 that, combined with all the historical, archaeological, and prophetic evidence, should make you confident that every part of it is absolutely true. "All Scripture is God-breathed." What does this mean? It is a simple and powerful promise that every word of the Bible is God's Word. He "breathed out" the words of the Bible through the pens of guys like the apostle Paul, Moses, David, Daniel, and John. Whether they knew it at the time or not, these men writing letters or poems or historical stories to friends, to fellow Christians, or for their own personal journals were writing the very words of God. The Spirit of God was guiding their hands, their minds, and their hearts so that every word written was what God intended. ⓑ

And the cool thing about God is that He used the writers' personalities, emotions, styles, and flairs in the writing of these books of the Bible. David writes like David, Moses like Moses, and so on. They weren't suddenly "possessed" by God in some "alien-force-took-me-over" moment as their pens just magically moved on the parchment and they wrote the words with glassy eyes. God used their everyday writing style in a supernatural way to accomplish an unprecedented thing: the communication of His words to humanity. ⑧

Here's another great verse. "Above all, you must understand that no prophecy of Scripture came about by the prophet's own interpretation. For prophecy never had its origin in the will of man, but men spoke from God as they were carried along by the Holy Spirit" (2 Peter 1:20–21). I want you to understand a couple of things from this passage. Notice the words "carried along." Those are the same words used to describe a boat that is being carried along by the wind in its sail. The idea is that the wind and the sail were working together in perfect harmony. The sail was "willingly" letting the wind do its work with no resistance. That's the same thing that happened with the writers of Scripture. They were the sail and God was the wind. They were working together in perfect harmony, and the result was a safe arrival in the harbor of God's perfect Word. ⑧

The next thing I want you to get about this passage is the very first sentence, "Above all, you must understand that no prophecy of Scripture came about by the prophet's own interpretation." What does this mean? It means that these guys didn't make it up. What they wrote is not fiction but fact. Every word of it is true. ⑧

GOD'S WORD PROVES ITSELF
TO BE TRUE

Now stop and think about this for a moment. God's Word proves itself to be absolutely true. Again and again through archaeological discoveries and fulfilled prophecy the Bible proves itself to be reliable. ⚙

Check out Josh McDowell's book *Evidence that Demands a Verdict* or Lee Strobel's *A Case for Christ* (the teen version) for more info on fulfilled prophecy, archaeological discoveries, and all sorts of cool stuff that shows Christianity is true . . . absolutely true. Ⓑ

Now, why is it important that we understand this? For the simple reason that if we can trust God in the subjects that we can scientifically test Him in (archaeology, history, prophecies, etc.), then we can trust Him in the areas where we can't scientifically test Him (spiritual warfare, salvation, end-times stuff, etc.). And if we can't trust Him in those testable areas, then we can't trust Him in the nontestable. ⚙

I want to reemphasize why this is important when it comes to spiritual warfare. If you don't approach the subject of spiritual warfare from this perspective, then one of two things could happen. First, you may reject it because some of the stuff you are going to hear is going to seem unbelievable. Second, if you don't look to God's reliable Book when it comes to the invisible reality of the dark kingdom, then you could be susceptible to all sorts of bad stuff. ⚙

You see, when it comes to spiritual warfare there are a lot of nuts out there. Some preachers misuse the Bible to tell all sorts of half-truths and outright lies when it comes to the devil. Their stories are interesting and often communicated with imagination and persuasion, but bottom line what they are preaching is not truth. ✿

So when you approach the subject of spiritual warfare, do so with the Bible in hand. When you hear something from someone about some aspect of the invisible reality, cross-check it with the Bible. Ask God through His Spirit to give you wisdom from His Word to show you what is the reality of God and what are the myths of mankind. Do the same as you read this book. Why? Because there is only one book that is completely true in everything it states (hint: it's not this one!). ✿

STAY CLOSE TO THE SHEPHERD

There is one other principle that I want you to understand before we begin this journey into the battlefield. It's this: "If you want to stay safe from the wolves, stay close to the shepherd." This is probably the most important truth you can keep in mind when it comes to the evil underworld that surrounds us. ✿

There is no magic formula for defeating the devil other than this . . . stay close to the Shepherd. The stronger the relationship that you build with Jesus, the safer you are from the Enemy's attack. Wander away from Jesus, even for a moment, and you become vulnerable to attack. ✿

I will never forget one day when I was driving home from the mountains with my wife. It was a beautiful Colorado late afternoon, and as we drove the winding mountain roads home I looked out the passenger side of the car. There I saw a herd of cows. Among the herd were a couple of calves wandering around. Nothing new. ✿

Then I saw a coyote sitting on its haunches a few hundred yards away. It was silent. It was watching. It was waiting . . . waiting for a calf to wander away. Waiting for a weak one to stray from the herd . . . waiting for dinner. ✿

Instantly I got a graphic reminder of the reality of spiritual warfare. Satan is waiting, watching, and hungry. He and his pack of wolves are circling the herd looking for strays. As soon as we wander away from Jesus we become vulnerable to his vicious attacks. Don't get me wrong, Satan will attack us even when we are in the fold of God's presence. The difference is that when we are close to Jesus, Satan can't hurt us. When we wander away from Him, then we have no spiritual armor to hide behind and no weapons to fight him with. ✿

How do you stay close to the Shepherd? Cultivate your relationship with God. Read His Word and think about it. Talk to God all the time. Journal your thoughts about God and your journey with Him. Ask Him to give you strength through His Spirit, who lives inside you every single day. Make Him the focus of everything you do. Play sports, do your homework, date (or court), and build friendships with Him in mind. As He becomes number one in your life, Satan can't defeat you. ⓑ

As a matter of fact, before we begin, let's make sure you are equipped with the most basic power source you need to win against the devil. Is the Spirit of God within you? Are you a child of God? You see, without God inside you have no chance to win against Satan. As a matter of fact, the Bible describes what Satan has done to you if you aren't a child of God. "The god of this age has blinded the minds of unbelievers, so that they cannot see the light of the gospel" (2 Corinthians 4:4). Has Satan blindfolded your spiritual eyes so that you cannot see the glorious light of the good news of Jesus Christ? How do you remove the blindfold? Actually the Spirit of God removes it and you simply believe the gospel message. ✸

That word gospel means good news. It is the good news that God made you to be in fellowship with Him. His purpose in creating you was to pour out His love on you and to be with you all the time as your King and your best friend. The problem is that you and I were born sinful and selfish. And because God is a holy God who hates sin, our sins separated us from Him. Our sin becomes a wall between us and God. And no matter how many good things we may do, those sins cannot be removed by good deeds. So you can go to church, go to Sunday school, go to youth group, and still go to hell. Now here's where the good news kicks in. ✸

Two thousand years ago God sent His only Son, Jesus Christ, into the world to become the perfect "God-man." And paying the price for our sin, Jesus died and rose again. He died in our place for our sin. He died for every sin you and I ever would commit past, present, and future. And then He conquered death and rose from the grave, proving that He was who He claimed to be . . . God in the flesh. ✸

Everyone who trusts in Him alone has eternal life. If you believe that Jesus died for your sin and you trust in Him alone to forgive you for all your sins, then you have eternal life. The key word is "alone." To be saved from the power of sin and Satan you must put your whole trust in Jesus Christ; not Jesus and water baptism, or Jesus and good deeds, but Jesus alone. He tells us in Ephesians 2:8–9, "For it is by grace you have been saved, through faith—and this not from yourselves, it is the gift of God—not by works, so that no one can boast." If we could get to heaven by good works, we would brag about it. We can't. The only way to heaven is through faith in Jesus Christ, so the only One we'll be able to brag about in heaven is Him!

If you are trusting in Him right now, then you have just received eternal life. Eternal life is a personal, permanent relationship with God that can never be broken by you and will never be broken by Him. It is a relationship that begins right now, not after you die. So if you are trusting in Jesus Christ for the first time, you can say this simple prayer to God: "Dear God, I believe that Jesus died for all my sins. I trust in Him alone to take me to heaven. I receive Your free gift of eternal life through faith right now. Thank You for forgiving me for all of my sins."

If you truly trusted in Jesus Christ, then you are going to heaven, not because you said some prayer, but because you believed in the only Person who could save you from an eternal damnation and a wasted life . . . Jesus Christ Himself. And guess what? He can save you from the power of the devil too.

As soon as you put your faith and trust in Christ, something powerful happened. In a very real sense Satan just lost the war for your soul. Here is what God's Word has to say about it, "Since the children have flesh and blood, he too [Jesus] shared in their humanity so that by his death he might destroy him who holds the power of death—that is, the devil—and free those who all their lives were held in slavery by their fear of death" (Hebrews 2:14–15). ✦

Not only that, but God has also equipped you with everything you need to win the battle against Satan. He has given you His Spirit. "And you also were included in Christ when you heard the word of truth, the gospel of your salvation. Having believed, you were marked in him with a seal, the promised Holy Spirit" (Ephesians 1:13). His Holy Spirit lives inside of you for good and is there to give you all of the power you need to defeat the Evil Overlord of the Underworld. ✦

If you put your faith and trust in Christ for the first time just now, welcome to the battle! Now before you read one more page of this book, go and tell your youth leader or pastor or a godly Christian adult what decision you just made! He or she will help you know the new Captain of your soul (Jesus!) better and prepare you for this fantastic and dangerous journey! ✦

Semper Fi

HOW TO USE THIS BOOK

This book is meant to be tribal. You can go through it as a youth group, an E-Team (you'll hear about that later), a campus ministry, or with a group of friends. You can even go through it as a family . . . yeah, yeah I know, but trust me it will work out. ✦

You could read it on your own and get a lot out of it, but this book is designed for you to read the chapters on your own and come together in some group setting to do the projects at the end of each chapter. One is a platoon project (to be done as a group) and the other is a personal project. If you are going through the platoon projects as anything other than a youth group, you may need to make a few adjustments to your project, but I'm confident that you'll figure it out. ✦

PLATOON CHALLENGES

 These are team projects designed to help you think through, understand, and apply the principles that you just learned in that particular challenge. Some of these are questions that you answer as a group. Others are projects that you do together. Most of these projects will take thirty minutes or more to do. ✦

AN ARMY OF ONE

 These are individual projects or questions that you do by yourself. They are designed to get you to "own" the material. If you are going to be prepared to do battle with the Evil One, then you need to take this stuff personally. ✦

The ultimate challenge, of course, is to live differently, pray intensely, and witness diligently as a result.

SOMEBODY HATES YOU

"Nothing short of the total destruction of the believer will ever satisfy our adversary."[1]

CHARLES SPURGEON

What would you do if you knew that outside, somewhere in the dark corners of your neighborhood, lurked a murderer? And, worse yet, he hated you. He concocted plans to nab you on the way to school or after practice or in the parking lot where you work. He is bigger than you, smarter than you, and can run faster than you. So, if you discovered his twisted plans, what would you do? The answer is simple. You'd do something: tell the police, rent a bodyguard, move out of the country . . . you would do something to stop him. Why? Because if you didn't you would be a statistic. ✹

I hate to be the bearer of bad news, but there *is* a superstalker out there who would love nothing more than to kill you. He hates everything about you. He hates who you are and what you do. And to make matters worse, he is not alone. He has a whole gang that numbers in the millions. Even the weakest members of his evil posse could shred you like paper. So what are you going to do about it? Something. ✹

By now you've guessed who and what I am talking about: Satan, demons, and spiritual warfare. Did you know that the Bible gives at least forty names and descriptive titles to the devil? From "accuser of the brethren" to "serpent" to "Son of the Morning," God paints a crystal clear picture of the Evil One so that you and I can be very familiar with this one who hates us so much. Before we learn how to fight him in the power of God's Spirit, we should take a few minutes and discover just who he is. ⓑ

You see, most Christians have their perspective of the devil shaped more by Hollywood movies than by God's holy Word. Movies like *The Exorcist, Evil Dead,* or even the dreaded Sauron in *Lord of the Rings* do more to affect our concept of Satan than the pages of the only fully reliable source of truth on this planet . . . the Bible. ⓑ

In the pages of this chapter we are going to discover just who Satan was before he became the devil, what he is like, how he turned bad, and why he hates us so much. So prepare your brain and your soul for a crash course on Satan. And remember, our answers aren't going to come from playing some cosmic guessing game or from hearsay. They are coming straight from God's Word. Here we go. ⓸

WHO WAS SATAN BEFORE HE BECAME "THE DEVIL"?

The devil wasn't always a bad guy. He actually started out to be astoundingly good and holy and wonderful. You may find that hard to believe, but here is what God's Word says about him: "You were the model of perfection, full of wisdom and perfect in beauty. . . . Your settings and mountings were made of gold; on the day you were created they were prepared. You were anointed as a guardian cherub" (Ezekiel 28:12–14). ⓑ

It's hard to believe, but this is how God described

Satan before he became Satan. In these three verses we see that Satan was God's ultimate creation, musical instrument, and personal bodyguard. ❂

SATAN WAS GOD'S ULTIMATE CREATION

Satan was one of a kind. Nobody else was like him in all of creation. No man, no beast, no other angel could compare. He was the "model of perfection." If God was taking you on a tour of all of His masterpieces and really wanted to impress you, He wouldn't take you to the most beautiful places on earth or the most amazing outer reaches of the universe. He would take you back to Satan before his fall into sin and amaze you with the view. You and I would be blown away. The one who someday would be called the Enemy of Heaven was once known as the masterpiece of God. ❂

SATAN WAS GOD'S MUSICAL INSTRUMENT

Yes, you read that right. He didn't play an instrument. He *was* an instrument. When the Bible describes his "settings and mountings made of gold," it is using Hebrew words for the parts of musical instruments. In the presence of God he rang out praises constantly. Like the fiery seraphim (a type of angel) in Isaiah 6, he was worshiping God nonstop. Many believe that He was the "choir director" for the rest of the angels in heaven. Before Satan started tooting his own horn, he was God's trumpet of praise. ❂

SATAN WAS GOD'S PERSONAL BODYGUARD

Remember the phrase, "You were anointed as a guardian cherub" from Ezekiel 28? It gives us a clue to who Satan was before he became the king of darkness that he is today. He was the protector of the throne of God. ✺

Now you may be thinking, *Why does God need a bodyguard? I thought He could protect Himself.* And you are absolutely correct. He doesn't need a bodyguard. But for that matter He doesn't need anything. He doesn't need worshipers. He doesn't need the universe. He doesn't need food or water or sleep. He is completely self-sufficient and self-existent. In other words, God is perfectly fine being God. But in His divine wisdom He made a universe and allowed a series of events where He could bring Himself the utmost glory. Part of His plan was to install His number one creation as His number one protector. Perhaps He installed Satan as His guardian cherub because of the sheer irony that His biggest protector would someday become His biggest enemy. God loves things like that. In the end when every knee bows and every tongue confesses that Jesus is Lord, it will seem fitting that Satan himself, the one-time protector of God's throne, will, once again, kneel and pay homage. ✺

WHAT IS HE LIKE?

OK. Before we begin I need you to erase from your mind every preconceived notion that you have of Satan. You know what I'm talking about . . . the kind of horned and fanged *Buffy the Vampire Slayer* version of Satan. Or maybe you have the medieval-looking, pitchfork-wielding, goatee-wearing kind of red devil action happening in your mind. ✸

WRONG!

THE MOST BEAUTIFUL
CREATION OF GOD

I don't know exactly how this picture of the devil became popular. Maybe it's because the book of Revelation refers to him as a dragon. But the book is simply being symbolic. The picture that is painted of the devil again and again is that of a beautiful creation of God, the most beautiful creation of God. Here is how 2 Corinthians 11:14 describes Satan, "And no wonder, for Satan himself masquerades as an angel of light." Finally, here is even more of the passage from Ezekiel that describes the devil as someone of amazing beauty: "You were the model of perfection, full of wisdom and perfect in beauty. You were in Eden, the garden of God; every precious stone adorned you: ruby, topaz and emerald, chrysolite, onyx and jasper, sapphire, turquoise and beryl" (Ezekiel 28:12–13). ✸

The stones that are mentioned here are only mentioned together three other times in all of the Bible. Two instances refer to the breastplate of the high priest in Exodus 28 and 39. The beautiful chest covering of the Old Testament high priest was so adorned because once a year he would go before the presence of God in the holy of holies. These stones were appropriate for the high priest to wear in the personal presence of God because they

reflected God's radiant glory in a wondrous kaleidoscope
of beauty. The final time these stones are mentioned in
the Bible is in the book of Revelation describing the New
Jerusalem. This beautiful city is described as made of
twelve layers of precious stones. Imagine the city of heaven
illuminated by the glory of God, brighter than the brightest
of suns. Talk about a dazzling array of colors too powerful for human eyes to bear! Talk about a kaleidoscope on
steroids! ⓑ

So why does God describe Satan as being adorned
with these same jewels? The use of these jewels to
describe Satan is not to say that he is literally made of all
of these beautiful stones or even that he is wearing them,
but to communicate his shining brilliance, his brightness
and beauty and luster. Satan is as brilliant and bright and
beautiful as the city of heaven itself! ☀

THE MOST INTELLIGENT
CREATION OF GOD

Now you may be thinking that Satan couldn't be all
that intelligent. I mean, after all, he tried to overthrow
God. But stop and think about it for a moment. Satan is so
intelligent that he runs an unseen government of rulers
and authorities (Ephesians 6:12) that, in turn, works
behind the scenes in every government on planet Earth,
including Capitol Hill. His government also pulls the
strings in Hollywood and Wall Street. He is constantly
planning and scheming to deceive, distract, discourage,
and destroy the staunchest and strongest of Christians
(1 Peter 5:8–9), while being able to simultaneously keep

the eyes of the lost blinded (2 Corinthians 4:4), the governments of the world colliding (Matthew 24:6–7), a myriad of false teachers organized (1 Timothy 4:1), and millions of demons busy (Revelation 16:14)! ✪

We use a small percentage of our brain's total capacity. He uses 100 percent of his (and he has a bigger brain!). Satan has mastered every verse of Scripture, every kind of philosophy, every strand of world religion, and every language on this planet. Einstein, Galileo, Da Vinci, and Bill Gates couldn't beat him in a game of chess or Trivial Pursuit on their best days. ✪

THE MOST POWERFUL
CREATION OF GOD

Satan is the most powerful creation of God. He is so powerful that God's new number one angel (Michael the archangel) wouldn't dare try to take on the devil by himself. Jude 9 makes this very clear, "But even the archangel Michael, when he was disputing with the devil about the body of Moses, did not dare to bring a slanderous accusation against him, but said, 'The Lord rebuke you!'" ✪

If God's biggest and strongest angel wouldn't dare take on Satan, what do you think the Prince of Evil could do to us? A fly would have a better chance of beating you up than you would have of beating Satan up by yourself. ✪

Sometimes I hear preachers who rant and rail against the devil. They call him names and treat him like he is some kind of junkyard dog that they could kick to death with no problem. Here's what the Bible says about these guys, "Yet these men speak abusively against whatever they do not understand; and what things they do understand by instinct, like unreasoning animals—these are the very things that destroy them. Woe to them!" (Jude 10–11). ✺

Let me sum up this verse: These kinds of preachers are idiots from God's perspective. They are talking boldly about things they don't know anything about. And God says that the results of their bold talk will be drastic action from God. Maybe He will turn His "junkyard dog" loose and see who gets the best of whom. ✺

What's the point for you? Respect his power. Don't go messing with the devil in your own strength. You may get a lion by the tail. ✺

LESSONS FROM THE LION'S CAGE

I will never forget one day in the zoo. I was with my wife and we were enjoying an afternoon at the Cheyenne Mountain Zoo in Colorado Springs. Hardly anybody else was there that day, so we were having a great time checking out the monkeys, gorillas (my favorite), giraffes, elephants, and, finally, the lions. ✺

Now the Cheyenne Mountain Zoo back then had a lot of cages and not a lot of glass enclosures. I liked that because we had a chance to get closer to the animals that way. ✺

We were alone in the lion area when we came into a big room with a gigantic male lion sleeping against the bars. I'll never forget how huge that lion was. Its big mane rested against the floor as it slept. And its tail was swinging back and forth *outside the bars!* As it swung back and forth, back and forth, I could almost hear it whisper to me, "Reach over the concrete barrier and grab me and see what happens. Come on, it will be fun, Greg. Just reach out and grab me!" ☀

My wife must have been able to hear the voice too, because suddenly she looked at me with those eyes and said, "Greg Stier, don't you dare! I know what you're thinking. If you grab that tail you are going to get in trouble." My response was simple, "What are they going to do, throw me in zoo jail?" With that I looked both ways to make sure nobody else was around, reached out, and grabbed that lion's tail with both of my hands. ☀

I don't know what I was expecting to happen. But something did happen . . . quick. That lion jumped up, turned around, and roared so loud that it reverberated through my entire body like a super subwoofer on the biggest speaker you could imagine. It was a sound like I've never heard or felt before or since. In that moment my heart was racing. In that moment my body was shaking. In that moment I almost lost control of my bodily functions. ☀

As I looked into his big brown eyes I could only see one thing . . . hatred. He wanted to shred me with his claws and then have me for lunch. He wanted to tear me from limb to limb. The only thing that saved my life that day was the bars. Because I couldn't have run if I wanted to . . . I was paralyzed with fear. ☀

Lessons? There are two. First of all, Satan is described as a roaring lion. First Peter 5:8 reminds us to "be self-controlled and alert [because] your enemy the devil prowls around like a roaring lion looking for someone to devour." He hates us. He wants to have us for lunch. The only thing that saves us every day from his claws and fangs is the grace of God. His love keeps the devil at bay and bars him from attacking us at will. We need to respect Satan's power and stay away from his cage. The second lesson: Husbands should listen to their wives. **ⓑ**

HOW DID HE TURN BAD?

So how did this awesome, powerful, beautiful, intelligent creation of God turn bad? How did someone so close to God become so far from God? How did God's highest creation become God's biggest enemy? How did Lucifer (his name before he sinned) become Satan? Believe it or not, the Bible gives a very specific answer. **ⓑ**

HE TOLERATED PRIDE
IN HIS HEART

Isaiah 14:12–14 says, "How you have fallen from heaven, O morning star. . . . You said in your heart, 'I will ascend to heaven; I will raise my throne above the stars of God; I will sit enthroned on the mount of assembly . . . I will make myself like the Most High.'" **ⓑ**

The sin of Lucifer started (as all sins do) as a sin of the heart. He said in his heart, "I will ascend to heaven; I will raise my throne above the stars of God; I will . . ." **ⓑ**

This was a sin of pride and conceit. You can tell by the words "I will" that are used over and over again. Have you ever heard somebody say, "I *will* ace my tests" or "I *will* win the game" or "I *will* get that girl" or "I *will* have my way"? These proclamations come from pride. There is only One being in the universe who can truly say "I will" and follow through every time. It's not you or me. It's not the devil. It is God Himself. ⬢

When Lucifer said "I will" in his heart, he was proclaiming his desire to be Lord of the universe in God's place. He wanted to rule over the stars of God (this term refers to the other angels of heaven). He wanted to sit in God's throne and be like God. ⬢

Who knows how this all started? Maybe one day he caught a glimpse of himself in a reflection of the gold of heaven and thought to himself, "Man, I'm good looking." Maybe he did a bodybuilder pose while admiring his powerful frame and thought, *There's no way any being in the universe could be stronger or smarter than me . . . not even God.* ⬢

Pretty soon he started making a plan in his head to overthrow God and establish himself as king. One by one he began recruiting angels to join him in his mutiny against heaven. ⬢

Ezekiel 28:16–18 describes how it happened, "Through your widespread trade you were filled with violence. . . . Your heart became proud on account of your beauty." ⬢

Those words, "widespread trade," describe how Satan recruited angels to defect from God's team to his. He promised to trade them rank and power in his new kingdom if they pledged to him their allegiance. Now, you may be thinking, *There's no way angels would join Satan in this insane conspiracy to oust God,* but you would be wrong. As a matter of fact Satan recruited one third of all of the angels to join him. ⬢

This goes to show how impressive Lucifer really was. One third of the angels of heaven thought that he would be successful in his quest to defeat God! Lucifer must have been a very impressive, powerful, beautiful, intelligent, and intimidating being. ◉

BUT THEN GOD FLEXED

God doesn't always flex His muscles. As a matter of fact, He is mostly patient and reserved. Maybe that's how the angels saw Him. Yes, they knew He was glorious. They knew He was awesome. What they didn't know, what they couldn't know, was the extent of His power. The angels who followed Lucifer in this unholy uprising mistook God's silence for weakness. But in the critical moment of confrontation God flexed, and Lucifer and one third of the angels were cast out of the presence of God. ◉

Lucifer became Satan. His followers became demons. The battle lines for all of human history were drawn. And sometime after that, we don't know exactly how long, Satan tempted Adam and Eve into sin. Second Corinthians 11:3 paints the picture clearly of what the devil did to Eve and does to us. "I am afraid that just as Eve was deceived by the serpent's cunning, your minds may somehow be led astray from your sincere and pure devotion to Christ."◉

Since Satan got evicted from heaven he is carrying out a vendetta on earth. His goal from the day Adam and Eve were created was to tempt them into sin and disrupt the plan of God for all of humanity to come. His goal from the day you were born has been to keep you in sin and disrupt God's plan for your life. And he is good at his job. ◉

WHY DOES HE HATE US SO MUCH?

The Bible describes Satan in Revelation 12:12 as a very angry being. "He is filled with fury, because he knows that his time is short." Now we can't be sure exactly why he hates humans, and especially Christians, so much. But I think there are at least three reasons for his uncontrollable rage toward us. ✺

I am convinced that the first reason he hates humans is that we were made in God's image and he wasn't. Remember from Isaiah 14 that he wanted to become like God? Well, his plan failed. But when God made Adam and Eve He created them in His image. Genesis 1:27 makes it clear that "God created man in his own image . . . male and female he created them." ✺

Being created in God's image means that Adam and Eve were like God, not in their power, knowledge, or omnipresence (a fancy word for the ability to be and see everywhere at the same time), but in their capacity for good, their ability to discern good from evil, their ability to rule over nature in an excellent and organized way, and their self-awareness and personalities. They were also able to feel love and compassion, to have a burning passion for the glory of God and a blazing hatred for sin. ✺

As impressive as Satan was, he was not created in the image of God. Adam and Eve were. I'm sure that hacked the devil. ✺

Another reason that I'm positive that Satan hates us is that we were made to rule the world. Speaking to Adam and Eve in Genesis 1:28 God says, "Be fruitful and increase in number; fill the earth and subdue it. Rule over the fish of the sea and the birds of the air and over every living creature that moves on the ground." ✸

God never gave the devil a world to rule and fill and dominate. Now here are these brand-new beings, Adam and Eve, naked and naive in the garden of Eden, and God gives them the kingship over this whole planet. This had to tick off the Evil One. ✸

The last reason I'm convinced that Satan is so mad, especially at Christians, is this: We received by grace what he failed to achieve by force. What do I mean by that? God has promised us that we will rule and reign with Him over this whole universe someday. He tells us in Revelation 22:5 that we will rule over this universe with Him forever and ever. By Jesus' side we will dominate heaven and earth, while Satan and his crew are burning in hell. ✸

So what does all of this mean for you? Somebody hates you. He is bigger than you, stronger than you, and smarter than you. He hates your guts, has got an army that numbers in the millions, and doesn't sleep at night. The only thing he does is scheme and connive to defeat Christians and derail the plans of God. ✸

So be on the lookout. Stand watch. As you read the rest of this book make sure that you put what you learn into practice. And whatever you do, don't grab this lion by the tail. ✸

PLATOON CHALLENGE

If Satan could write a letter to your youth group, what do you think he would say? Write it out as a letter. Then imagine what Jesus would say, and write a letter to combat the devil's letter. Read your letters and discuss as a group.

AN ARMY OF ONE

Take five minutes and ask God to give you the strength that you need to win against this powerful enemy who hates you so much.

2

ARMOR ALL

*1 super power,
5 pieces of gear, and
1 unstoppable weapon
to use against the devil*

inally, be strong in the Lord and in his mighty power. Put on the full armor of God so that you can take your stand against the devil's schemes. For our struggle is not against flesh and blood, but against the rulers, against the authorities, against the powers of this dark world and against the spiritual forces of evil in the heavenly realms. Therefore put on the full armor of God, so that when the day of evil comes, you may be able to stand your ground, and after you have done everything, to stand. Stand firm then, with the belt of truth buckled around your waist, with the breastplate of righteousness in place, and with your feet fitted with the readiness that comes from the gospel of peace. In addition to all this, take up the shield of faith, with which you can extinguish all the flaming arrows of the evil one. Take the helmet of salvation and the sword of the Spirit, which is the word of God. And pray in the Spirit on all occasions with all kinds of prayers and requests. With this in mind, be alert and always keep on praying for all the saints. (Ephesians 6:10–18)

It was probably the strangest and scariest thing that ever happened to me. I was a sophomore in high school on a date with my girlfriend late on a Friday night. We were at a festival with thousands of other people. Most of them were drinking, riding rides, and having a good time. We were having a great time as well, but we were witnessing. We talked to other teenagers, invited them out to youth group, and shared the good news of Jesus. Things were going pretty well until that fateful decision. ●

I'm guessing it was around ten o'clock at night when we decided to get a breather from the big crowd. It was getting close to the time I needed to get her back home anyway. As we walked down a dark side street in the basic direction of where the car was, I noticed a house that had been converted into some kind of store. Above the door in big letters were the words "ABRA CADABRA." I was thinking that this was some kind of magic trick store or something. It was open and the lights were on. I talked to my date and asked her if she wanted to go in and check it out. She didn't. She said she thought it looked creepy. But I persisted. After a few minutes she hesitatingly agreed, and we made our way up to the stone sidewalk to the "creepy" house-turned-store. ●

As I pushed the screen door open and walked in, I knew that I had made a mistake. It was almost as though I could feel the presence of something dark, sinister, and evil in the room. What we saw next sent chills down our spines. There in the middle of the big room was a table filled with all sorts of weapons. Not guns, but clubs, knives, swords of all sorts stretched across the long table. There must have been at least twenty different weapons right in the middle of this "magic store." The weapon I noticed immediately was closest to me. It was a mace (not the kind you spray). This large club dwarfed the other weapons on the table. It was huge, and on the hurting end of the shaft was a large heavy ball with sharpened blades protruding from it. One swipe from this huge weapon would drop somebody for good. ●

At the time I was studying martial arts and was intrigued with this huge weapon. I immediately picked it up and was impressed by how big, heavy, and sturdy it seemed. My girlfriend stood behind me, right by the screen door, ready for a quick escape. That's when I noticed *them:* two big, creepy looking men leaning against the opposite wall. They were twice my size and didn't look real friendly. I guess they worked there, because one of the guys dressed in all black asked, "Can we help you with something?" ✪

"Yeah," I answered. "What are all these swords and stuff here for?" ✪

I'll never forget his answer. "Oh. Some are for fighting. Some are for show. Some are for *sacrifices and rituals.*" ✪

When he mentioned "sacrifices and rituals," I heard the screen door fly open and the sounds of my girlfriend running out of the house. She had seen and heard enough. I wasn't quite ready to leave. I knew that Jesus was at my side (and that big mace was within my reach). So I asked the question, "What religion are you?" ✪

He answered without hesitation, "I'm a pagan." ✪

Now true paganism is kind of a mix between witchcraft, New Age mysticism, and some aspects of satanism. In ages past pagans often made animal and human sacrifices as part of their rituals. I was getting scared when the big man asked the inevitable question, "And what religion are you?" ✪

The words just came out, "I'm a Christian." ✪

Suddenly his demeanor changed. It was almost as though some evil power took control of him. In a deep and angry voice filled with hatred he yelled at me, "Don't you know that Christ died two thousand years ago?" Without hesitating I asked, "Don't you know that He rose again from the dead three days later?" He didn't like that answer. ✸

By this time he and his friend had inched their way up to the opposite end of the weapon-filled table. The memory of what happened next is etched forever in my brain. He picked up the sword closest to him and bellowed to his friend, "This is the perfect sword for killing a Christian" and started walking toward me. ✸

Have you ever been so scared that all the hair on your neck stands on end? Try that times ten. I was absolutely petrified. Now there were a lot of options at my disposal at that moment that I could have (and probably should have) acted on. I could have simply run out the screen door and caught up to my girlfriend. There is no way they could have caught me—I was fueled by adrenaline and sheer terror. I could have dropped to my knees and called out to God for help. To be honest, I should have run. There are times we make stupid decisions that endanger our lives. This was one of those stupid things. Instead I picked up the mace, wielded it back like a baseball bat, and yelled, "And this would be the perfect weapon for killing a pagan! Let's get it on!" ✸

He stopped cold in his tracks and turned ghost white. Why? Was he intimidated by my hulking 150-pound frame? No. Was he terrified by the size of my biceps? Probably not (seeing as my girlfriend had bigger biceps than me). No. He stopped his charge in absolute fear because my weapon was bigger than his. My mace was twice the size of the puny sword in his hands. ✸

He stopped in his tracks and dropped his sword. I dropped my mace and ran for the screen door. What's the lesson? There are two. First, I reacted badly to his threat of force. I should have run. Christians aren't called to violence but love (Oops!). Second, when fighting Satan on a spiritual level (which we are called to do), we have the advantage, not because we are bigger or stronger, but because our weapons are bigger. ✹

When we take Satan on using the weapons that God has provided, he will drop his weapons and run every time. ✹

That's what this chapter is about, the weapons and armor and power that God has provided us to do battle with the devil. ✹

THE ONE REAL SUPERPOWER

Spiderman has the ability to cast webs and climb walls. Superman is able to leap tall buildings in a single bound. Storm can induce hurricanes in the blink of an eye. The Incredible Hulk has tremendous strength. Every superhero has a super power. Some of them have cool gadgets, and all of them have awesome outfits (like Batman and his plasto-abs), but without their super powers, they are pretty vulnerable. ✹

God gives us an awesome superhero outfit and all sorts of cool gadgets in our battle with the powers of darkness. Some are protective. Others are weapons. But without our super power we are in trouble. ✹

Before the Bible lists the gear and gadgets, it tells us about our super powers. In Ephesians 6:10 we are commanded to "be strong in the Lord and in his mighty power." ✴

Now here's the great thing about our super power. It's not ours but God's! When we trusted in Jesus Christ as our Savior we received the ability to be transformed in and through the personal power of God Himself. ✴

The strength it took for God to raise Jesus from the dead and establish Him as king of the universe (Ephesians 1:19–21) is the same power available to us! What does this mean? It means that when we are allowing God's power to surge through us, there is not a villain on the planet, a sin in our lives, or a problem with our relationships that cannot be fully defeated. ✴

Maybe you're not quite getting this . . . God is making all of His power available to you to live your life victoriously. How powerful is God? According to Colossians 1:16–17, He created the universe, and He holds the universe together every day. Scientists talk about how subatomic particles called "quarks" are the glue of the universe. They are the particles that make atoms and molecules stick together. But there is a quirk behind the quark that scientists don't usually talk about. It is the fact that God's power is truly the glue of the universe. If He were to lift His hand off the cosmos, even for a split second, everything and everyone everywhere would fall apart. ✴

God's power is nothing to mess with. It is indescribable and unimaginable. The only thing God can't do is sin. So His power will help you become victorious over any sin. ✴

I come from a family filled with bodybuilders and power lifters. Many of my uncles and cousins have won awards for their physique and strength. I have not been blessed with those same genes. Yes, I work out. No, I can't even come close to what my family can squat, curl, or press. ✳

There have been times in the gym that I wished that just for one day I could have all of their strength coursing through me. I can imagine stacking the plates on the bar until it bends and then, with all of the gym-goers watching in awe, taking that huge weight and pressing it over and over and over again. OK, so I'm living in a dream world. Or am I? ✳

Although I'll never be able to bench-press half of what my uncles and cousins can, I am able to have all of the strength of God Himself coursing through the biceps and triceps of my soul. Through His strength I can bench-press any problem that comes my way. And so can you. ✳

The first and most important truth to realize when it comes to putting on the superhero suit of armor God has provided you is this . . . it all starts with getting filled, empowered, and controlled by the strength of God Himself. How do you do that? Confessing any known sin in your life, you ask God to take control of you. It's as simple as that. ✳

FIVE PIECES OF PROTECTIVE GEAR

Contact sports require protective gear. Try playing football without a helmet and you'll get my point. Spiritual warfare is a contact sport. It is a hand-to-hand, face-to-face encounter with someone bigger, stronger, faster, and meaner than us. So if you try to take on the devil without your armor on, then all bets are off . . . you lose.

God gives you five pieces of gear to wear to protect and prepare you for your battle against the forces of darkness. These pieces of armor are listed in Ephesians 6:13–17. Each piece of armor is a unique and absolutely essential part of the gear God has provided you so that no part of your life can be injured by the devil. Think of these pieces of armor as a superhero suit that you put on every day. You know what I'm talking about . . . like Batman and Robin's full-body, plasto-abs protective suits, complete with bat-boots, bat-gloves, bat-mask, and bat-belt.

Let's take a look at each piece and see what it protects and how it works.

THE HOLY HELMET OF SUPER SALVATION

"Take the helmet of salvation" is the command God gives us. Salvation is one of those words that kind of sounds spiritual, but most people don't really know what it means. It simply means deliverance or the act of saving someone. Let's say that you are walking down the street and you see a big man beating up a little girl. You want to stop him, so you jump between him and her and tell the man to stop. He does. What just happened? Salvation! You became a "savior" to that little girl. You delivered her from the beating. You saved her from his fists. In the same way we were getting beat up by sin. It was bruising us with crushing blows when Jesus stood between us and took sin's biggest punch in

our place. What just happened? Salvation! Jesus became our Savior. ✪

So the holy helmet of super salvation is the power of God that protects us from sin. Because Christ stood in for us, the penalty of our sin was paid in full and the power of sin is broken for good. We can walk in spiritual victory over sin when we strap on our headgear. What does a football helmet do? It protects a player's head from crushing blows. What does the helmet of salvation do? It protects our mind and thoughts from the power of sin so that Satan cannot deceive us into living like we're not saved. ✪

Maybe there is a sin in your life that is so powerful, so engaging, so addictive that you think you can't have victory over it. Maybe it's a sexual or drug addiction. Maybe it's a gossip habit or unresolved anger. Whatever it is, know that when you strap on your headgear it doesn't stand a chance. But you must believe that the power of God has delivered you from the beating that sin is giving you. You must believe that Jesus stood in and took the punch from that habit for you when He died on the cross. ✪

THE BULLETPROOF BREASTPLATE OF RIGHTEOUS RIGHTNESS

"Stand firm then . . . with the breastplate of righteousness in place" (Ephesians 6:14). ✪

God's breastplate protects your heart from sin. In the Bible a person's heart represents the person's motives and

ARMOR ALL / 47

internal life. As Satan shoots his bullets and swings his blades at you, if your heart is protected by the cover of righteousness, then you are safe. What is righteousness? Look at the root word *right* for a clue. Think of righteousness as rightness. It is the rightness of God provided to us through Jesus Christ. ✹

Now would be a good time for a crash course in theology. In the Bible there are two kinds of righteousness before God. There is legal righteousness and real-life righteousness. One smacks of a courtroom and the other a classroom or locker room or your room (places where real life happens). ✹

When you trusted in Jesus Christ as your Savior you were justified. This means that you were "declared righteous" in the courtroom of God. The Bible says in Romans 3:22, "This righteousness from God comes through faith in Jesus Christ to all who believe." ✹

You believe and you receive. You believe and you are declared right in the courtroom of God. None of your past, present, or future sins will be held against you. God no longer sees your sins. He sees the bloodied cross of Christ and all of your sins nailed to it for good. God sees you through blood-colored lenses. And because the blood of Christ washes your sins away, God doesn't hold your sins against you in His courtroom. ✹

What if you were a murderer condemned on death row, waiting to die in the electric chair? Imagine the fear in your heart as your day of execution came closer. As that fateful day ended, you ate your last meal, said your last prayers, and marched under close guard to the chamber where you would soon die. Just before they strapped you in, the door burst open and a man screamed, "No! Don't strap him in, because I am taking his place." As he was being tied down you asked him the question, "Who are you?" His answer is almost unbelievable. "I am the judge's son. I volunteered to die in your place. You have been declared legally right by my father, and I'm taking your punishment so that you can live. You are free to leave this prison." ✺

Sound unbelievable? Well that's exactly what happened when Jesus died on the cross. He's the Judge's Son who died for all of us who are criminals against heaven. We are declared right because Jesus took our wrong. And now we are free to live and leave the prison of sin. That's where real-life righteousness comes in. ❸

Could you imagine being that condemned murderer who was forgiven and pardoned completely, and then leaving the prison to start randomly killing, raping, and robbing again? How could someone who received such forgiveness spit in the face of the law so boldly? It's no different for us. When we are declared right in the courtroom of God and freed from the prison of sin, we are called to live a new life that pleases God. If we don't live a right life, we are spitting in the face of the God who freed us. ❸

So strap on the bulletproof breastplate of righteous rightness. Live a life that pleases Him. Protect your heart and your motives. Ask God to transform the legal righteousness of Christ into real life rightness in the things you do everyday. As you protect your heart, Satan can't drive his dagger into your soul by causing you to go back to a life of crime against heaven. ✺

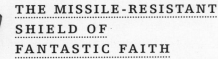

THE MISSILE-RESISTANT SHIELD OF FANTASTIC FAITH

Did you ever play gladiator as a child? I did. Using broom handles as swords, my friends and I would have beaten each other to death if it weren't for the trash-can-lid shields. Each blow was diverted, deflected, and defeated by the old reliable and smelly trash can cover. If a friend swung his broadsword in my direction, it was easily stopped. If he threw something at me, all I had to do was lift up my shield and block it.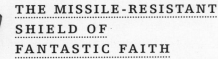

God has given you a shield so that you can protect yourself from Satan's attacks. "Take up the shield of faith, with which you can extinguish all the flaming arrows of the evil one." The picture here is Satan launching flaming missiles in your direction as you hide behind this shield of fantastic faith. What are the missiles? They are Satan's lies. He wants you to buy his lies so that he can discourage and defeat you.

For some of you guys those lies revolve around what being a man is really all about. Satan is launching his offensive against you through missiles that mislead. He is telling you lies like,

"Real men bench-press more."

"Real men hang out with the in crowd."

"Real men date the hottest girls."

"Real men wear the coolest clothes, drive the best cars, and have the best jobs."

For some of you girls those lies revolve around your self-image. Satan's missile launch against your soul is fueled by lies like,

"You're way too fat."

"Other girls are prettier than you."

"You'll have to puke your way to a better body."

"If you give him what he wants, he'll love you." ✪

So when Satan shoots his lies at us, what do we do? We lift up the shield of faith. It represents the promises of God that we claim through faith. When Satan tells one of you guys that "real men bench-press more," you lift up the shield of faith by quoting verses like 1 Timothy 4:8, "For physical training is of some value, but godliness has value for all things, holding promise for both the present life and the life to come." When Satan tells one of you girls that "you're way too fat," you lift up the shield of faith by quoting verses like Psalm 139:14, "I praise you because I am fearfully and wonderfully made." You see, there is one guy in this universe who thinks you are drop-dead gorgeous. He is the "guy" who made you . . . Jesus Christ! ✪

What does all this mean? It means that you have got to start getting to know (by heart) some of the promises of God. This means that you learn the discipline of verse memory. Think of it like this: The more verses you know and can quote, the bigger your shield is. If you, like the typical Christian in America, have only two verses memorized, then your shield is probably the size of a salad plate. The more promises of God you memorize, the less Satan can get his misleading flaming missiles past your defenses and into your soul. ✪

Listed below are some flaming missiles from Satan and some of the faith-shield verses that God has to block them. ✪

WHICH LIES DO YOU BUY?

SATAN'S LIES

GOD'S PROMISES

SATAN'S LIES	GOD'S PROMISES
"NOBODY LIKES YOU!"	"This is love: not that we loved God, but that he loved us and sent his Son as an atoning sacrifice for our sins." *1 John 4:10*
"YOU HAVE GONE TOO FAR FOR GOD TO FORGIVE."	"When you were dead in your sins and in the uncircumcision of your sinful nature, God made you alive with Christ. He forgave us all our sins . . . " *Colossians 2:13*
"YOUR LIFE HAS NO PURPOSE."	"Now get up and stand on your feet. I have appeared to you to appoint you as a servant and as a witness of what you have seen of me and what I will show you." *Acts 26:16*
"YOU ARE TOO ADDICTED TO EVER STOP."	"You have been set free from sin and have become slaves to righteousness." *Romans 6:18*
"YOU'LL LOSE ALL YOUR FRIENDS IF YOU GET SERIOUS ABOUT JESUS."	"Am I now trying to win the approval of men, or of God? Or am I trying to please men? If I were still trying to please men, I would not be a servant of Christ." *Galatians 1:10*
"GOD CAN'T USE YOU."	"But God chose the foolish things of the world to shame the wise; God chose the weak things of the world to shame the strong." *1 Corinthians 1:27*

Just think about it. If you memorized one verse a week for one year you would have fifty-two verses memorized. Talk about a big shield! ✸

THE BATTLEFIELD BOOTS OF SHARING-YOUR-FAITH READINESS

I'll never forget the first time I put on a pair of cleats. As soon as I walked out onto the turf I felt invincible. Why? Because I could dig my feet deeply into the sod and get ready for the ball to be hiked. As soon as it was hiked I was off, and it didn't matter if the grass was wet, because my cleats were sinking deep beneath the blades of grass into the mud below. Cleats give a feeling of readiness and stability. That's exactly what the battlefield boots of sharing-your-faith readiness does. It prepares you to stand firm in whatever situation you are in and be ready for the slippery task of sharing your faith with your friends. ✸

God tells us to have our "feet fitted with the readiness that comes from the gospel of peace." Simply put, this means to be ready at all times to share your faith. Are you ready? Do you know how? If so, when's the last time you told somebody about Jesus? If you're not ready, why not? You wouldn't play a full-contact football game without shoes on, so why would you live life without your battlefield boots on? Strap up and get ready to share your faith. ✸

Walking down the mall and seeing a teenager's shirt got my attention. In big white letters on a black T-shirt were the words, "I'd rather go to hell than go to school."

I walked right past him into the store—after all, I was in a hurry. With each passing step the Spirit of God convicted me. His T-shirt was a wide-open opportunity to share the gospel with that teen. But instead of asking him about his T-shirt and moving the conversation to spiritual things I chickened out. I ran back into the main corridor of the mall and looked for him, but he was gone . . . and so was the opportunity. My boots weren't buckled. My cleats were hanging up in the locker room of self-absorption. By the time I got them on, the battle had passed me by. ✿

As I was walking out of the mall to my car, I thought about how many opportunities I've missed because my boots weren't on. My question for you is this: How many are you missing? Every day we have opportunities to share our faith. All we must do is open our eyes and seize the moment. So buckle up your battlefield boots of readiness every day and get ready to strike when the opportunity arises. ✿

THE UTILITY BELT OF TOTAL TRUTH

"Stand firm then, with the belt of truth buckled around your waist." Sometimes when I work out with really heavy weights (heavy for me anyway), I put on a gigantic belt called a weight belt and cinch it up as tight as I can. This big leather belt gives me back support and makes me feel like I can lift whatever weight is put on the bar. Some of it is psychological. Some of it is real. But something about this big belt brings safety, security, and confidence. The same is true of the big belt of total truth.

This piece of our superhero outfit provides safety, security, and confidence. We cinch it up and it gives us real support in our battle against evil. We buckle it tight and it brings everything together. ⬢

It's called the "belt of truth" because it represents truthful living. When somebody tells a lie, he says something that is false. It doesn't measure up to reality. When a Christian lives a lie, he is not measuring up to the reality of who he is in Christ. ⬢

God call us to practice what we preach. He calls us to be consistent, whole, and truthful in the way that we live. The belt of truth could be called the belt of integrity. ⬢

The words *integrity* and *integer* are closely related. You've heard of an "integer," haven't you? For those of you who failed mathematics, here's what an integer is: "A complete entity; a whole number, in contradistinction to a fraction or a mixed number." An integer is a whole number. When we are people of integrity, we are whole people. We are not fractioned in thought or divided in spiritual loyalties. So get whole. As we grow toward becoming spiritual "integers" there will be no divisions between our beliefs and behaviors, no fractions in our commitment to Christ, no multiplications of our focus. We will be all about Jesus. So you do the math in your own life and I'll do it in mine. How's it adding up in your spiritual walk? ⬢

The belt of truth is the belt of integrity. It is the centerpiece of your protective gear. It gives you wholeness as a person and strength of character to face the onslaught of attacks you are bound to face as a Christian teenager.

It protects the guts of who you are from hypocrisy or succumbing to the temptations of the Evil One. How do you put it on? You choose to be the same person at church, at youth group, at school, and in your room. D. L. Moody, a famous evangelist who lived a hundred years ago, said, "Character is what you are in the dark." So who are you when nobody else is looking? Tighten your belt and get it together.

ONE UNSTOPPABLE WEAPON: THE INDESTRUCTIBLE SWORD OF THE SPIRIT

"Take the . . . sword of the Spirit, which is the word of God" (Ephesians 6:17). ✸

With all of this talk of armor and protective gear, it's easy to forget that God has armed you with a weapon as well. This powerful sword is the same weapon that Jesus used against Satan when he tried to tempt Jesus to compromise in the wilderness. It is the Word of God. ✸

Now before you think I'm talking about carrying a Bible with you wherever you go so that you can bust it out against the devil anytime he tempts you, think again. The Bible is not telling us to carry the Bible in our backpacks but in our hearts. You see, in Greek (the original language that the New Testament was written in) there are two words for "word." One means the written word. The other means the spoken word. In this passage when God tells us that the Indestructible Sword of the Spirit is the Word of God he is telling us that it is the *spoken* Word of God. ✸

What does all this stuff mean? It simply means that you must begin to study the Bible and begin to memorize verses that can be instantly recalled to memory and spoken out loud if you expect to beat the devil down. David put it this way in Psalm 119:11, "I have hidden your word in my heart that I might not sin against you." David knew that if he was going to have victory against sin and Satan, then God's Word must be in his heart and on his lips. ⬤

There is something about God's Word that cuts the devil to the core. He hates it. It slices through his defenses and pierces him deeply. In the midst of a temptation or trial, we need to recall the verses that we have put to memory and speak them aloud. When we do, Satan and his demonic army can't stand against us. ⬤

Hebrews 4:12 puts it this way, "For the word of God is living and active. Sharper than any double-edged sword, it penetrates even to dividing soul and spirit, joints and marrow; it judges the thoughts and attitudes of the heart." The Word of God is a powerful weapon. No weapon formed against it, in the seen or unseen world, can stand against it and survive. ⬤

WHAT THIS MEANS

This means that if you expect to be victorious against the devil, then you must be putting God's Word to memory on a consistent basis. I have heard that the average Christian in America knows two verses by heart. That doesn't surprise me. Most Christians don't take time to memorize verses. Verses like John 3:16 and Genesis 1:1 represent the full arsenal of verses that the typical Christian knows. ⬤

What if every verse was one inch of the blade of your sword? How big would your sword be? Would you have a pocket knife or a broadsword to swing at the devil? ⬡

The great thing about this generation of teenagers is that they want to do something significant and they are not afraid of hard work. Well, that's great, because I'm going to give you something significant and hard to do, and that is to start a memory verse program that will help you to have fifty-two verses committed to memory at the end of a year. I am asking you to commit to memorizing one verse per week for an entire year. At the end of that year your blade will be sharp and ready to swing at your spiritual enemy in the power of the Spirit of God. ⬡

HOW DO YOU MEMORIZE A VERSE?

Here's how I have done it for years. I take a 3 x 5 card and write the verse on one side and the verse reference on the other. Then I take that card with me everywhere I go. I repeat every phrase several times until I can say it without looking, then I move on to the next phrase and do the same. I do this until I can join all of the phrases together without looking. Finally I say that verse several times out loud and repeat the reference every time I say it (so that I know the verse and the reference by heart). I then repeat the verse at least five times every day for the rest of the week. Then the next week I begin another verse. At least once during that week I also recall the verse I memorized the previous week. Once I get more than one verse, I punch a hole in the corner of the 3 x 5 cards and put a ring binder through the hole so that I can have all the verses together. ⬡

Below are listed fifty-two verses that every Christian should know and the subjects they deal with. You can memorize your own verses or use my suggested list (or mix and match), but the challenge stands . . . fifty-two verses in one year. Now that's a sword! And by the way, if you want to make sure this gets done, don't do it alone. Get at least one friend (if not a group of friends) to make this commitment with you. ✸

JOHN 3:16 . . . gospel

GALATIANS 5:16 . . . spiritual growth

PSALM 119:11 . . . verse memory

JOHN 10:10 . . . hope

1 THESSALONIANS 4:3–4 . . . sexual purity

ROMANS 6:1–2 . . . victory against sin

EPHESIANS 6:12 . . . victory against Satan

MATTHEW 28:19 . . . sharing your faith

JOHN 10:28 . . . eternal life

JEREMIAH 33:3 . . . prayer

PSALM 63:1 . . . passion for God

PHILIPPIANS 3:10 . . . knowing Jesus

2 CORINTHIANS 5:10 . . . Judgment Day

JOHN 14:6 . . . Jesus—the only way

ROMANS 12:1 . . . total surrender

JAMES 1:22 . . . obeying God's Word

1 PETER 3:15 . . . defending your faith

EPHESIANS 1:13 . . . the Holy Spirit

JOHN 10:30 . . . Jesus is God

JOSHUA 1:8 . . . meditating on God's Word

ECCLESIASTES 9:10A . . . working hard

EPHESIANS 2:8–9 . . . salvation not by good deeds

JOHN 14:2 . . . heaven

REVELATION 14:11 . . . hell

HEBREWS 4:16 . . . confident prayer

1 JOHN 5:13 . . . confidence in our salvation

GALATIANS 6:7 . . . sin's consequences

GENESIS 50:20 . . . God's plan for good

ROMANS 3:23 . . . everyone sins

GALATIANS 2:20 . . . crucified with Christ

GALATIANS 1:8 . . . watch out for false gospels

COLOSSIANS 4:2 . . . commitment to prayer

PHILIPPIANS 2:3 . . . humility

ACTS 1:8 . . . witnessing

2 TIMOTHY 3:16 . . . God's Word

1 SAMUEL 16:7B . . . God's perspective

PSALM 101:3 . . . hating sin

EPHESIANS 6:10 . . . God's strength

DEUTERONOMY 6:4 . . . one God (Trinity)

MATTHEW 3:16–17 . . . three Persons (Trinity)

JOHN 15:5 . . . connection to Jesus

JAMES 1:2 . . . dealing with trouble

1 CORINTHIANS 1:18 . . . the power of the Cross

TITUS 3:5 . . . good works aren't enough

1 CORINTHIANS 15:3–4 . . . Jesus' death and resurrection

ROMANS 6:11 . . . dead to sin

2 CORINTHIANS 4:18 . . . eternal perspective

2 PETER 1:3 . . . everything we need

DEUTERONOMY 6:5 . . . loving God

EZEKIEL 22:30 . . . God looks for somebody

ROMANS 8:28 . . . God works things out

PROVERBS 15:1 . . . stopping arguments

These verses will give you a good start to a lifelong memory verse program. My challenge to you is to read God's Word, think about it, take notes in your Bible, absorb it, and let it soak through your soul. Memorizing these verses will be a good start to sharpening your sword. ✪

HOW DO YOU PUT ALL
THE ARMOR ON?

OK, you have your holy helmet of super salvation, your bullet-proof breastplate of righteous rightness, your missile-proof shield of fantastic faith, your big belt of total truth, your battlefield boots of witnessing readiness, and your indestructible sword of the Spirit. Now how do you put it all on? Easy . . . pray. Depend on God for the strength to go into battle with the armor He has provided. ✹

Right after God lists out all of the pieces of the armor He tells us to "pray in the Spirit on all occasions with all kinds of prayers and requests" (Ephesians 6:18). The very act of prayer is how we put all of our armor on. You see, prayer is an act of dependence on God. When we pray we are telling God, "I can't do this on my own. I need You." As we depend on Him, He takes control of us with the Spirit, our super power is ready to flex, and our armor is automatically in place. That's why He tells us to pray "in the Spirit." That means that we are fully controlled, empowered, and outfitted by God's Spirit, who is dwelling in us. ✹

Not only do we pray for ourselves, but we pray for other believers. "With this in mind, be alert and always keep on praying for all the saints" (Ephesians 6:18). We pray for other believers here and across the world to be fully empowered and armored in their battle with Satan. ✹

And what is the goal of all of our prayers? The advancement of the kingdom of God through winning souls from the dark domain of Satan. Paul wrote, "Pray also for me, that whenever I open my mouth, words may be given me so that I will fearlessly make known the mystery of the gospel" (Ephesians 6:19). After explaining the battle against Satan and listing all of the pieces of armor and weapons at our disposal in the battle against Satan, Paul asked the believers in the city of Ephesus to pray for him to have courage to share the gospel. Paul knew that the whole goal of the battle was to rescue lost souls from behind enemy lines. In the heat of this bloody battle Paul wanted a fearless intensity that would enable him to share the gospel without trembling. We need the same dose of boldness in the battle for our friends. Sure, sharing your faith can be scary, but God can give you the courage to overcome your fears and reach your friends. Just ask Him for it. ✹

PLATOON CHALLENGE

Break up into six groups and each take one of the following
pieces of the spiritual armor and the one unstoppable weapon.
Do a short skit on how you can use that piece of armor in an
everyday life situation. If the total number of you is fewer than
twelve, take more than one piece per group.

1. Holy Helmet of Super Salvation

2. Bulletproof Breastplate of Righteous Rightness

3. Missile-Resistant Shield of Fantastic Faith

4. Battlefield Boots of Sharing-Your-Faith Readiness

5. Utility Belt of Total Truth

6. The Unstoppable Weapon:
The Indestructible Sword of the Spirit

AN ARMY OF ONE

• Write out a prayer to God asking Him to energize you
with His super power every single day. Remember that
every time you pray you are depending on God to give you
the superhero strength you need to beat down the devil!

• My Superhero Prayer . . .

3

THE ULTIMATE SMACKDOWN

The rock ain't got nothing on the Rock!

Have you ever seen a professional wrestler up close? I will never forget the day I did. It was late in the afternoon and I was on my way into the gym where I work out. As I was walking in I looked up to see a wall of a man. He was about six foot eight and had to weigh close to four hundred pounds. He was the biggest man I have ever seen. Now I come from a family of title winning bodybuilders and power lifters (although I somehow missed that gene), so I'm used to being around big men. But you could have fit two of my family members in each of this guy's thighs. He was doing curls with seventy-five-pound dumbbells effortlessly and was military pressing more than three hundred pounds. As he walked through the gym, it became silent. The only thing we could hear were the reverberation of his feet against the floor as he pounded the ground toward the big weights. Everyone was in awe. The next-biggest guy in the gym picked up all of his stuff and left. He didn't want to stand anywhere near this gigantic man. Later I found out that this man was a professional wrestler in town for a match. **⊛**

As I watched this man I thought to myself, *If I got into a fight with him I wouldn't stand a chance.* He was too big, too strong, and too mean for me to take on (not that I would want to!). **⊛**

The same is true of Satan. He is a raging demon on spiritual steroids. He is bigger, stronger, and meaner than any man on the planet. No muscle-ridden tough guy would ever stand a chance against him. There is only one person in human history who is stronger . . . Jesus Christ Himself. ✿

In this chapter we are going to explore the four different matches that the Bible describes between Jesus and the devil. Three of these battles were in the past. One is yet to come. The lesson at the end of the chapter may change your life forever. So let's take a look at each of these bloody matches between Jesus and Satan. ✿

THE RUMBLE BEFORE THE JUNGLE (EZEKIEL 28:11–19)

In 1974 Muhammad Ali met George Foreman in Zaire to determine who would be the boxing heavyweight champion of the world. To the surprise of many, the older, smaller Ali knocked out George Foreman in the eighth round. Boxing fans have nicknamed this classic match "The Rumble in the Jungle." ✿

Long before this classic match there was another heavyweight fight I like to call The Rumble Before the Jungle. This was a battle between Jesus and Satan before the jungle of sin had corrupted the heart of humanity. Before Satan got Adam and Eve booted out of the jungle called Eden through temptation and trickery, Satan got kicked out of the splendor of heaven by the pride of his heart. ✿

In Luke 10:18 Jesus said, "I saw Satan fall like light-ning from heaven." In other words, when Satan sinned, he got thrown out of the ring so fast that he hit the earth like a lightning bolt. When Satan's conspiracy to take over heaven was found out, Jesus threw him over the turn-buckles of the heavenly city and into the stands. It really wasn't much of a fight. Satan and his fellow wrestlers were cast to the earth with a single devastating move from Jesus. ✹

Now this doesn't mean that Satan has lost all access to heaven. We know from Scripture that Satan regularly appears before the governmental throne of God and gives reports (Job 1:6–7) and accuses Christians (Revelation 12:10). He is consistently before God's throne pointing out our faults and giving reports to God. But he has lost access to heaven as his home. Instead planet Earth is his main domain. ✹

THE WILD WILDERNESS BATTLE (MATTHEW 4:1–11)

Then Jesus was led by the Spirit into the desert to be tempted by the devil. After fasting forty days and forty nights, he was hungry. The tempter came to him and said, "If you are the Son of God, tell these stones to become bread." Jesus answered, "It is written: 'Man does not live on bread alone, but on every word that comes from the mouth of God.'" Then the devil took him to the holy city and had him stand on the highest point of the temple. "If you are the Son of God," he said, "throw yourself down. For it is written: 'He will command his angels concerning you, and they will lift you up in their hands, so that you will

not strike your foot against a stone.'" Jesus answered him,
"It is also written: 'Do not put the Lord your God to the
test.'" Again, the devil took him to a very high mountain
and showed him all the kingdoms of the world and their
splendor. "All this I will give you," he said, "if you will bow
down and worship me." Jesus said to him, "Away from me,
Satan! For it is written: 'Worship the Lord your God, and
serve him only.'" Then the devil left him, and angels came
and attended him.

The Wild Wilderness Battle is the only bout that
lasted three whole rounds. Jesus was hungry, weak,
and tired. He hadn't eaten for forty days straight. When
Jesus was at His weakest physically, that's when Satan
attacked Him. ⚙

What does this teach us about the devil's tactics? He
does his best work when we are at our weakest. Satan
fights dirty. Maybe it's after a long, hard day and you are
alone in your room exhausted, and BAM! he attacks with
the temptation of Internet pornography. Maybe it is after
an emotionally draining breakup that he whispers in your
ear thoughts of suicide. Satan pulls no punches and he
kicks when you're down. ⚙

Satan offered Jesus shortcuts to three things that
Jesus wanted. His goal was to get Jesus to flex His divine
muscles to get what He wanted earlier than God the
Father planned it. Satan knew that if he could get Jesus to
bite on any of these temptations, then God's will would be
bypassed and God's Son eliminated from being the death
sacrifice for the world. Let's take a look at each of these
temptations and compare them to how Satan tempts us to
take shortcuts in our lives. ⚙

SHORTCUT TO SATISFACTION

"After fasting forty days and forty nights, he was hungry. The tempter came to him and said, 'If you are the Son of God, tell these stones to become bread.'" Imagine going for forty days without food. You would be starving . . . and so was Jesus. So many times we think of Jesus as less human than we are. WRONG! Jesus was fully God and fully human. In other words He was mad hungry. And He was God. He could have whipped up a Big Mac with fries, a pepperoni pizza, or an ice cream sundae with a snap of His fingers. Satan knew that, and so he dared Jesus to turn the stones in the middle of this wasteland into piping hot heavenly bread. ◉

But Jesus was not finished with His fast until the Father told Him that He was finished. During this fast Jesus had been feasting on the Word of God, so He told Satan, "It is written: 'Man does not live on bread alone, but on every word that comes from the mouth of God.'" Jesus had better bread to munch on . . . the Word of God. Although His stomach was growling, His soul was satisfied. ◉

How many times has Satan tempted you to take a shortcut to satisfaction when it comes to your appetites? The whole condition of bulimia is built on this shortcut. Girls want a shortcut to weight loss, so they purge and puke their way to a "better" body. Guys want sex and God wants to let them have it . . . in the context of marriage. But instead of guys' waiting for the rings and the preacher pronouncement, Satan tempts them to take a shortcut to sex in the backseat of a car or a hotel room on prom night. ◉

SHORTCUT TO POPULARITY

This may surprise you, but Jesus' whole goal is to be popular. Now it's not the same kind of self-centered philosophy that you and I think of when the word *popular* is used. It is a good kind of popular. It is the kind of popularity that is fitting for the Ruler of the universe. The Bible calls this popularity "glory." Jesus prays in John 17:1, "Glorify your Son, that your Son may glorify you." He wants to be famous so that He can make His Father famous. So this particular temptation from Satan was especially appealing. "Then the devil took him to the holy city and had him stand on the highest point of the temple. 'If you are the Son of God,' he said, 'throw yourself down.'" ☀

Jesus knew that it would just be a matter of time before He was finally recognized by the Jews as the true Messiah, the One sent by God to rescue them from their enemies. When Jesus returns to this earth the second time, He will be famous. He will finally be recognized by all the world for who He really is . . . God Himself. ☀

But Satan was asking, "Why wait that long, Jesus? Why not get the popularity You deserve right now? Imagine the response of the Jewish leaders if You jump off the top of the temple and all of the angels of heaven rush to catch Your body on the way down so that You land on Your feet unscathed and unhurt. They will bow before You as the King that You are. Why wait for the fame? Take what's Yours right now." ☀

What was Jesus' response? "It is also written: 'Do not put the Lord your God to the test.'" In other words, it isn't really smart to give God a dare. ☀

What about you? Are you trying to take a shortcut to popularity? Are there jokes you shouldn't laugh at but do because you want to stay in with the "in" crowd? Are there students who probably aren't the best influence that you hang with in the hopes that you will be accepted? "I dare you to shoplift this CD." "I dare you to smoke this." "I dare you to _____" (fill in the blank). Just remember popularity with the posse is nothing compared to popularity with God. If you choose to live a life full for God, then there will be a day when you "receive a rich welcome into the eternal kingdom" (2 Peter 1:11). So don't take a shortcut to applause. Heaven's standing ovation is infinitely better than what your friends think of you. ✹

SHORTCUT TO POWER

Someday Jesus will rule and reign completely and supremely on this earth. Under His direct rule this world will be a totally different place. But until then, God has allowed Satan to oversee the earthly domain. Don't get me wrong, God is ultimately in control of this world. Nothing happens apart from His will. But, in His divine will, He has chosen to let Satan rule the world for a short time. ✹

In the final bout of the Wild Wilderness Battle, "the devil took him to a very high mountain and showed him all the kingdoms of the world and their splendor. 'All this I will give you,' he said, 'if you bow down and worship me.'" Jesus never argued, "It's not yours to give." He didn't say, "I am already ruling this world." Why? Because Satan could have given complete authority over the planet to Jesus to let Him immediately rule! There was only one condition: Satan wanted Jesus to bow His knee and worship him. ✹

Once again the devil was offering a shortcut, this time to power. Someday, way off in the future, Jesus would rule and reign on this earth. Satan was offering Him all of the power right then. ✹

Jesus responded by quoting the Bible again, "Away from me, Satan! For it is written: 'Worship the Lord your God, and serve him only.'" The devil left. ✹

Satan also offers you shortcuts to power. If you're a football player, maybe that shortcut to power is the temptation to take steroids. You've been pumping iron and eating protein, but it's just not packing on the mass you think you need to be a better lineman, linebacker, or whatever. "Just three months' worth of shots and you will build muscles that you couldn't build in three years at the gym," Satan whispers in your ear. "Take the shortcut." ✹

Or maybe it's a shortcut to a different kind of power. You know that to get that powerful job you are going to need a powerful degree from a powerful college. But first you have to get past that test. You could study hard and risk your future on the strength of your memory, or you could take the shortcut . . . cheating. ✹

Whatever your particular shortcut temptation is, just remember that God is calling you to take the long road to success and "power." He wants to use the blood, sweat, and tears of trial and testing to mold you into the servant of God He calls you to be. Like Jesus, quote God's Word, surrender to God's Spirit, and say, "Away from me, Satan!" ✹

Three and out. Satan tried three times to pin Jesus and couldn't. This leads to an interesting question, "Could

Jesus have given in to sin?" The answer is no. Jesus has a divine nature (He is God) and a human nature (He is man) but no sin nature. We are born sinful humans because of the spiritual sin "gene" that was passed on to us through our parents and grandparents all the way back to Adam. But Jesus was conceived by the Holy Spirit. He had no sinful nature as a man. And as God, He is incapable of sin. ◉

The natural question is "Then why did Satan tempt Jesus?" First, the devil is not the sharpest tool in the tool shed when it comes to estimating the power of God. Remember he thought that he could overthrow God in the beginning. He thinks that he can overpower God at the end. Is it unreasonable to think that Satan thought, *If I can get Jesus to sin, then God's whole plan will unravel?* Second, it was God's will that Satan tempt Jesus. Remember that it was the Spirit of God who led Jesus out to the wilderness so that He could be tempted. God wanted to show the world that even under direct attack from the strongest created being in the universe (Satan himself) in the worst possible conditions (in the desert) and the weakest physical condition (after a forty-day fast), Satan couldn't make a sin dent in the Son of God. ◉

This should encourage us, because when we are tempted we know that we have a God who relates! No matter what you are going through, Jesus went through more . . . and endured . . . and He shows us how to endure the temptations and trials that we face in our lives. ◉

We succeed against the devil's temptations to take shortcuts the same way Jesus did. We depend on the Spirit, we quote God's Word, and we resist the devil. ◉

THE JERUSALEM GRUDGE MATCH
(COLOSSIANS 2:13–15)

When you were dead in your sins and in the uncir-
cumcision of your sinful nature, God made you
alive with Christ. He forgave us all our sins, having
cancelled the written code, with its regulations, that was
against us and that stood opposed to us; he took it away,
nailing it to the cross. And having disarmed the powers and
authorities, he made a public spectacle of them, triumphing
over them by the cross.

It looked like Satan had Jesus pinned. I mean after all,
there was the body of the Son of God twisted, mangled,
and nailed to a cross of wood. The screaming crowd was
mocking Him as the heel. But what looked like a sure win
for the Evil One was the end of Satan's power. ✹

When Christ died He pinned the powers of darkness
once for all. According to Colossians, "He made a public
spectacle of them, triumphing over them by the cross."
What does that mean? It means that Satan and his demonic
army were humiliated in absolute embarrassing defeat by
what took place on Calvary two thousand years ago. ✹

The death of Christ was really the end of Satan's
career. Yeah, he had a few more battles to fight, but the
war was ultimately over. Jesus crushed his power by
destroying the sin principle once and for all. ✹

The Jerusalem Grudge Match wasn't much of a
match at all. As a matter of fact God's Word predicted
hundreds of years before that Satan would suffer a loss at
the foot of the cross. In rebuking Satan (represented by the

serpent in Genesis chapter 3) God said, "And I will put enmity [hatred] between you and the woman, and between your offspring and hers; he will crush your head, and you will strike his heel" (Genesis 3:15). In this verse the serpent's offspring represents Satan, and Eve's offspring represents Jesus. During ancient crucifixions the heels of the victims were often bruised due to the weight of their bodies being fully placed on the heels of their feet as they were suspended on the cross. But the bruising of Jesus' heel resulted in the crushing of Satan's head. The idea is that of a person stepping on the head of a snake in the grass and crushing it until it dies. What the Romans did to Jesus by crucifying Him was nothing compared to what Jesus did to Satan! His evil power was once and for all crushed at the Cross. When we choose to walk in the power of the resurrected Jesus who lives in us, there is no way that Satan can pin us! ✸

THE BRAWL TO END IT ALL
(REVELATION 20:7–10)

There is one last battle. It is the Brawl to End It All! At the end of the ages the Bible describes this final wrestling match between Jesus and the devil. ✸

When the thousand years are over, Satan will be released from his prison and will go out to deceive the nations in the four corners of the earth—Gog and Magog—to gather them for battle. In number they are like the sand on the seashore. They marched across the breadth of the earth and surrounded the camp of God's people, the city he loves. But fire came down from heaven

and devoured them. And the devil, who deceived them, was
thrown into the lake of burning sulfur, where the beast and
the false prophet had been thrown. They will be tormented
day and night for ever and ever. ✸

After one thousand years in fiery exile, Satan will
be released to wreak unholy havoc on the earth. He will
gather all the rebellious of heart in every nation and
surround the city of Jerusalem to destroy Jesus and the
people of God. Bad idea. Satan just doesn't learn. He got
whaled on thousands of years ago and thrown out of the
ring in heaven. He lost again in the Wild Wilderness
Battle. He really got beat down at the Cross, and this is the
last straw. Fire comes down out of heaven and destroys
them all completely. Satan is thrown into the flames of the
lake of fire where he will burn forever and ever. There will
never be a pardon or parole. He will burn for eternity.
Game over. Jesus wins . . . again. ✸

What does all of this mean for you? If you are on
Jesus' team, you are on the winning team. Maybe you
have been picked last and laughed at first all of your life.
That's OK. In the end, you and I and Jesus will get the last
laugh on Satan. When you signed up to be a Christian, you
signed up on the winningest team of all time. Our Savior
is undefeated and undaunted. We can live in victory as we
keep our eyes on Him. No sin, no demon, no problem, no
person, no habit, no teacher, no parent, no friend, no
memory, nobody . . . can defeat you. If you stay by Jesus'
side and draw your strength from Him, there is no losing.
Jesus is 4 and 0! ✸

PLATOON CHALLENGE

Get in a big circle, then ask and answer these questions:

1. Why do you think Satan was so set on overthrowing God in the Rumble Before the Jungle?

2. In what ways do we try to overthrow God in our daily lives?

3. How are the three temptations that Satan attacked Jesus with similar to temptations that he attacks us with? Share specific examples.

4. How did Jesus' ultimate defeat of Satan at the Cross affect our battle against Satan and sin?

5. How should the future final defeat of Satan by Jesus make us feel today? (Use one-word answers for this one.)

AN ARMY OF ONE

In what areas of your life is Satan smacking you down? Be honest and specific.

THE BIGGEST BULLY AT YOUR SCHOOL

"So Satan went out from the presence of the Lord and afflicted Job."

JOB 2:7

lmost everybody has a story of a bully who terrorized him in some way growing up. Maybe it was that older elementary school student who used his height and size to give you a swirley in the restroom. Maybe it was the wedgey from the football player who looked like he was on steroids and acted like he was on crack. Maybe it was that girl who was so mean that you planned your journey to the next class the long way so that you could avoid her in the hallway.

I think of Robbie in elementary school, Steve in junior high school, and Bruce in the years that followed. Big, bad bullies. But as big as they seemed at the time, they don't even come close to the biggest bully in the history of humanity. You guessed it . . . Satan!

SATAN'S ATTACK ON JOB

There is a whole book in the Bible that deals with his intimidating ways. It's the book of Job. Satan stole Job's lunch money, attacked his family, and beat him up bad. And what's worse is this . . . God let it all happen.

What does all of this have to do with you? Everything! Satan wants to bully you as well. And at times God will let it happen. This chapter takes a look at the bullying tactics of the devil and why God will sometimes let him swing his fists at you. So let's take a look at what Satan did to Job. ⓑ

The LORD said to Satan, "Very well, then, everything he has is in your hands, but on the man himself do not lay a finger." Then Satan went out from the presence of the LORD. One day when Job's sons and daughters were feasting and drinking wine at the oldest brother's house, a messenger came to Job and said, "The oxen were plowing and the donkeys were grazing nearby, and the Sabeans attacked and carried them off. They put the servants to the sword, and I am the only one who has escaped to tell you!" While he was still speaking, another messenger came and said, "The fire of God fell from the sky and burned up the sheep and the servants, and I am the only one who has escaped to tell you!" While he was still speaking, another messenger came and said, "The Chaldeans formed three raiding parties and swept down on your camels and carried them off. They put the servants to the sword, and I am the only one who has escaped to tell you!" While he was still speaking, yet another messenger came and said, "Your sons and daughters were feasting and drinking wine at the oldest brother's house, when suddenly a mighty wind swept in from the desert and struck the four corners of the house. It collapsed on them and they are dead, and I am the only one who has escaped to tell you!" At this, Job got up and tore his robe and shaved his head. Then he fell to the ground in worship. . . . In all this, Job did not sin by charging God with wrongdoing. (Job 1:12–20, 22)

In seconds Job discovered that he had lost everything and everyone dear to him. His wealth was wiped out and his children were dead. He had been attacked by the biggest bully of human history, Satan himself. Let's take a look at how this bully beat Job down. **Ⓑ**

SATAN STOLE HIS LUNCH MONEY

The first thing Satan did was to have Job's oxen and camels stolen and all of his sheep burned up with fire. Now you have to understand that in ancient times a person's net worth was determined by how much land he owned and how many oxen, camels, and sheep he could put on that land. Wealth was determined not by the size of a person's mutual funds, but by the size of his herds. Satan wiped out Job's portfolio in moments. **Ⓑ**

Job went from being one of the wealthiest men in town (he had thousands of sheep) to one of the poorest men around in nothing flat. Satan took his lunch money. **Ⓑ**

SATAN ATTACKED HIS FAMILY

Within seconds of discovering that his net worth was jack squat he heard the most devastating news of all—all ten of his grown children had died suddenly in a catastrophic windstorm. I can't imagine the pain of losing my only son, let alone ten children in one day. But there was more destruction to come. **Ⓑ**

SATAN BEAT HIM UP BAD

After Job successfully endured this trial without getting mad at God or cursing His name, Satan asked God to let him attack Job's body. Here's what happened. "So Satan went out from the presence of the LORD and afflicted Job with painful sores from the soles of his feet to the top of his head. Then Job took a piece of broken pottery and scraped himself with it as he sat among the ashes" (Job 2:7–8). ⬢

Have you ever had a big zit that hurt so bad that all you wanted to do was pop it to relieve the pressure? Imagine huge boils that covered your body from head to toe. With every square inch of your body a pussy pustule of pain, you would just want to die. The only relief that Job could get was to take broken pieces of pottery and scrape away the pus from his seeping sores. ⬢

Even though his wife begged him to curse God and die, Job refused. He recognized that God was God and as God could do whatever He wanted . . . even if Job didn't understand. And he didn't understand. Job had no idea what was going on behind the scenes. He had no clue that this was an extreme case of spiritual warfare from the highest ranking general in the army of darkness. All he knew was that everyone he loved was dead, everything he had was gone, and every part of his body was bursting with pain. ⬢

The bully beat him down, stole him blind, and left him to rot. And God let it all happen. ⬢

Why would God let this happen? ⬢

This is the question that plagued Job for the rest of the book. Three friends who had heard of his tragedy came to visit him so that they could comfort him. At first they sat in silence and hurt with their beloved friend. But when Job began to complain to them about his unjust suffering, their comfort turned into confrontation. ⬦

Each of Job's "friends" took turns verbally attacking Job and accusing him of doing something drastically sinful. Their reasoning went that God is just, and because He is just, then tragedy and trouble come from God when we sin. So Job must have done something extremely bad to deserve such a punishing blow from God. He argued with each of them. This is when Job veered into sin head-on. Instead of sitting in silence he lashed back against his friends and defended his personal integrity. Pretty soon he was accusing God of unjustly attacking him. Job 3 through 37 sound like a courtroom drama as each party argued his case with logic, intensity, and emotion. ⬦

GOD'S REASONS FOR ALLOWING THE ATTACK

This went on and on and on until God finally showed up, rebuked Job and his friends, and basically said, "I'm God. You can't figure Me out. Deal with it. And, oh, by the way, ask Job to pray for you so I don't pour out My judgment on you." ⬦

So the question remains . . . why did God let all of this happen to Job? There are at least three reasons. ⬦

A HIGHER PURPOSE

God had a higher purpose that, as far as we know, Job never knew about . . . to prove to Satan Job's faithfulness in the midst of the most painful situations in life. In chapter 1 of Job, God was bragging about Job's commitment to Him. Just like a father who is proud of his son, God was proud of Job and let Satan know about it in no unclear terms, "Have you considered my servant Job? There is no one on earth like him; he is blameless and upright, a man who fears God and shuns evil" (Job 1:8). Satan told God that the only reason Job served the Lord was that He had put a hedge of protection around him and blessed all of his work. So God allowed Satan to tear apart Job's life. But Job still didn't sin or question God. ✹

So in chapter 2 God stuck Satan's nose in it again, "Have you considered my servant Job? There is no one on earth like him; he is blameless and upright, a man who fears God and shuns evil. And he still maintains his integrity, though you incited me against him to ruin him without any reason" (v. 3). The first reason that God let Satan bully Job was to show Satan up. He knew that Job was faithful. He knew that Job was committed to Him. He knew that if Satan did his worst on Job that Job would stand strong . . . and he did. ✹

There may be some trials that you are going through that you just don't understand. "Why would God let my girlfriend/boyfriend break up with me after we've been going out so long?" "Why would God let my mom get cancer?" "Why would God let me have such bad acne?" "Why would God make our family move again?" ✹

You may never know (in this life anyway). But know this . . . there is a God who knows why, and He has a higher purpose. Maybe He is showing you off in front of the kingdom of darkness and saying to Satan, "Have you seen my servant (your name here)?" **⬢**

A DEEPER REASON

At the end of the book of Job, God took Job and his friends on a verbal tour of the universe and the earth. He asked them if they were tough enough to fight off God's biggest and baddest animals. He asked them if they understood the universe and its workings. He asked them if they could even begin to understand His infinite wisdom and ways. **⬢**

What was Job's response? **⬢**

"Surely I spoke of things I did not understand, things too wonderful for me to know. . . . My ears had heard of you but now my eyes have seen you. Therefore I despise myself and repent in dust and ashes" (Job 42:3, 5–6). **⬢**

Job learned the lesson: God is God, Job is not. God does what God does, and God is right no matter what because He is God. The best thing Job could do is sit in silence with his hand over his mouth and trust in God no matter what. **⬢**

One of my best friends is a guy named Danny Oertli. I've known Danny for years. He is the worship leader at our Dare 2 Share student conferences. On the road he is my roommate. We talk, pray, dream, hang out, and have a really good time. His wife, Cindy, and my wife, Debbie, were friends as well. Sometimes when we weren't traveling on the road, the four of us would get together for dinner and have a great time. Then Danny got a taste of a very personal Job experience. On February 4, 2001, Cindy suddenly died of a heart attack. At the time I was on vacation with my wife at Disney World. I'll never forget that day as my phone rang and Danny sobbed out between the tears, "Cindy's dead. What do I do?" I collapsed to the sidewalk and cried with my friend on the phone. I had no idea what to say to him, with the love of his life gone for good from this earth. He lost someone more important to him than all the wealth of this world suddenly, unexpectedly, and tragically. ⊕

Over the weeks and months that followed I saw my friend struggle to go on and, sometimes, even to breathe. But he forced himself to go on. Often he would have to leave the room to go outside and cry. But not once did I see him lose faith in his God. He never wavered in his trust in the Lord. In the deepest season of his grief, his eyes turned upward. I learned how to endure an overwhelming trial from watching my friend Danny. You can learn as well. ⊕

If you are a Christian, then remember that whatever problem you are faced with, God is bigger. Whatever person may forsake you, God will not. Whatever you think of yourself, God loves you unconditionally. Whatever you have messed up, God can restore. Whatever hole you have in your soul, God can fill it. ⊕

He has a deeper purpose for the pain He brings into your life. He wants to make you like Jesus. And if you want to be like Jesus, then you have to learn how to pick up your cross of pain and follow in His blood-stained footprints. The way of the cross is the way of pain. But

God uses that pain to forge and form us into the image of Christ. ✺

If you want to embrace your God, then embrace your pain. It is the master sculptor's chisel that removes all of the excess stuff that is keeping you from being transformed into the likeness of Christ. Chisels hurt. Embrace your pain. ✺

A BIGGER PLAN

I love the book of Job because it tells a no-holds-barred story of one man's personal journey of suffering. I also love it because God doesn't give all of the answers to all of the suffering. And that's the way life is. We never have all of the answers for everything. Nobody likes to be around those who think they do. ✺

For more than ten years I was a preaching pastor at Grace Church in Arvada, Colorado. I can't count the number of funerals I have officiated. Oftentimes I conducted those services with other pastors. Sometimes they would try to comfort grieving family members with token answers of why God allows suffering and pain, loss and grief. More often than not those grieving loved ones would look back with hollow eyes of hopelessness that seemed to whisper, "Preacher, you have no clue of what I'm going through. Keep your theories to yourself." ✺

I learned early on not to give easy answers, because there were none. What do you tell a mom who lost her baby two days after birth? What do you tell a father who just lost his beloved teenage daughter when the drunk in the oncoming traffic swerved and hit her car head-on? What do you tell a Danny Oertli? ✺

Although there are no easy answers to the suffering we go through, there is one benefit—we can help others who are going through the same thing. Danny was able to comfort a mutual friend, Ryan Ward, when he lost his lovely wife, Cadi, unexpectedly just months after Danny lost Cindy. Danny comforted Ryan in a way I could not. ✺

The book of Job does the same thing for you and me. Job was able to endure the full fury of the devil, and so can we. Countless believers have drawn comfort from its pages through their darkest times of suffering. Without the story of Job, the Bible would be incomplete. The element of real pain in the real world by a real person would be missing to a large degree. God let Job go through all of his stuff for us! Through it we can understand how God uses suffering for His own divine purposes. And we have an Old Testament character to relate to when it comes to trouble and trial. ✺

Job relates to our suffering and, more important, so does Jesus. As much as Job went through, Jesus suffered more. And now He is at the right hand of God interceding to God on our behalf. He knows what you are going through. He empathizes with your pain. God's Word reminds us that "we do not have a high priest who is unable to sympathize with our weaknesses, but we have one who has been tempted in every way, just as we are—yet was without sin. Let us then approach the throne of grace with confidence, so that we may receive mercy and find grace to help us in our time of need" (Hebrews 4:15–16). ✺

LESSONS FROM THE BEATING

There are four lessons I want you to take away from this chapter.

SATAN CANNOT ATTACK US WITH OUT A PERMISSION SLIP

Each time Satan attacked Job he needed a permission slip from God. Satan reminded God that He had placed a hedge of protection around Job so that Satan couldn't get to him. The deceiver then begged Him to trim back the hedges so that Satan could get at Job. God said yes. But oftentimes God says no. ✸

In Luke 22:31–32 Jesus told Peter, "Satan has asked to sift you as wheat. But I have prayed for you." [Satan DID get a yes here too.] In other words, "Satan wants to pull a Job on you, Peter, but don't worry, I have prayed for you, and the Father always answers My prayers." ✸

The Bible paints a picture of Satan in Revelation 12 as an "accuser of our brothers." He is consistently before God's throne picking out our flaws and asking God for persecution permission slips. Sometimes God says yes, and sometimes God says no. It is not random. Every time He says yes to Satan's request God has a higher purpose, deeper reason, and bigger plan. ✸

GOD WILL NOT LET SATAN ATTACK
US WITHOUT A PURPOSE

Remember that every "bad" thing that comes into your life is a gift from God. He is using His chisel to chip off the sin until you look like Jesus to the watching world. He knows that your suffering now could be used to minister to others in pain later. And, who knows? He may be using your example to show you off in front of the forces of darkness. Maybe He is so confident of your faithfulness that He is going to allow that bad thing so that he can rub Satan's nose in it when you pass the test with flying colors! ✺

WE MAY NEVER KNOW WHAT
GOD'S PURPOSE IS WHILE WE
ARE ON EARTH

As far as we know Job never knew about the whole satanic dynamic in his personal suffering. He didn't mention Satan in any of his talks, and God didn't bring it up in His lecture to Job and his friends. ✺

In the same way, we may never know why God lets us go through all of the pain on this planet. Someday, on the other side of eternity, we will know why. As 1 Corinthians 13:12 reminds us, "Now we see but a poor reflection as in a mirror; then we shall see face to face. Now I know in part; then I shall know fully, even as I am fully known." Back then mirrors were made of polished bronze, so they weren't that good. It would be kind of like looking at your reflection in a lake on a windy day. ✺

Have you ever looked in one of those mirrors that magnify? It kind of freaks you out (or me anyway), because you can see every single zit in all of its magnificent glory; every pothole and crease stand out in a stark reminder of your facial flaws. Someday we will be able to look into God's magnifying mirror of human history. We will see every reason for every trouble and trial. We will understand the whys behind the whats for the very first time. Until then we trust in God no matter what, knowing that He knows the whys. ✪

IN THE END ALL BELIEVERS WILL LIVE HAPPILY EVER AFTER

"The LORD blessed the latter part of Job's life more than the first. He had fourteen thousand sheep, six thousand camels, a thousand yoke of oxen and a thousand donkeys. And he also had seven sons and three daughters" (Job 42:12–13). ✪

After the trial of the century God blessed Job again. His wealth was multiplied. His portfolio restored. His honor regained. Now he had twenty children (ten on earth and ten in heaven), and it was "all good" again. He lived happily ever after. So will we. ✪

Whatever you are going through just now, when it is all said and done, God will bless you and restore you and prosper you. It may not happen on this earth, but it will happen. Plenty of believers throughout history died penniless and suffering, but now they are blessed. The poorest believer in heaven is richer than the richest person ever to live. Because we are children of the King, we will receive His kingdom someday . . . and all of the riches in it. We can't even guess the rush of unspeakable joy, the thrill of indescribable worship. The adrenaline of seeing the Creator, the crucified, the King of Kings will be reward enough for anything we've been through. ✹

So don't worry about whatever has been worrying you. The pleasure is worth the pain. The joy of heaven is worth the hells we endure in our darkest days. Like Job we will live happily ever after. ✹

PLATOON CHALLENGE

As a group create a modern day Job story.
Develop characters for every part of the story and then
perform it in front of another group (your whole youth
group, the church, whoever). Have the youth leader or
student leader develop a talk that goes with it.

AN ARMY OF ONE

In what three areas is the devil bullying you in your life?

1. _____

2. _____

3. _____

5

SATAN'S HOME BOYS

"Demons have always been active in the world since the dawn of human history."[1]

LEWIS SPERRY CHAFER

Thomas really freaked me out. He claimed to see things I couldn't. He thought he knew when somebody nearby was possessed by a demon. When Thomas talked like that it made me wonder about him. Was he for real? Did he have some God-given power to see into the spiritual realm that I did not? Was he faking it? Or was something, or worse yet someone, more sinister behind his insights into the invisible? ✷

Just months earlier Thomas had a radical conversion to Christ from satanism. My good friend Donnie and I were working a booth at a crowded annual gathering in Denver called The People's Fair. Ours was one of hundreds of booths that went up at the civic park right smack dab in the middle of downtown Denver every summer. Well over one hundred thousand people would come to this weeklong event and visit booths that sold food and crafts. Some booths promoted atheism, witchcraft, New Age mysticism, or, in our case, Christianity. ✷

Donnie and I and others would pass out gospel tracts to those who came by our booth, answer questions, and engage them in conversations about spirituality. Sometimes people would trust in Christ. Sometimes people would reject Christ. It was exciting to meet and talk to so many people about Jesus. ✷

I had just left Donnie to man the booth when somebody from another Christian booth came running up to
him saying, "We've got this guy at our booth who claims
to be demon-possessed. Every time we mention the name
of Jesus he throws up. We need your help. We are trying
to cast this demon out and don't know what to do!" Now
you have got to know Donnie to appreciate this story. He
is a big, bodybuilding, no-nonsense Italian guy who is
absolutely in love with Jesus and an evangelist at heart.
His first question was, "Have you tried sharing the gospel
with this guy?" Their response was "No. Every time we
mention the name Jesus he pukes." He said, "Well, go get
a bucket, because he's about to hear a lot about Jesus." ⓑ

Donnie didn't waste any time. He shared the gospel
with Thomas. And, finally, after Thomas threw up a few
times, the message of the gospel got through, and Thomas
believed. His first words were "The demon is gone." After
years as a satanist, after years of being terrorized by a
demon, Thomas was freed. How? Was it through an
intense exorcism? Was it by a highly ritualized series of
confrontations mixed with holy water and Latin phrases?
No. It was through the power of the gospel of Jesus Christ.
When Thomas believed the gospel, Jesus burst in, threw
the demon out, and took control of Thomas's soul. ✸

Months later I was in a restaurant with Thomas trying
to help him grow in his newfound relationship with Christ.
He told me, "Do you see those two guys at that table?" ⓑ

"Yes," I said.

"They have demons of homosexuality."

"How do you know that?" I asked.

"I can sense these demons" was his response.

"Thomas, let me ask you a question. Do you ever worry that your 'ability' to see into the spiritual realm may be Satan's way of getting a spiritual stronghold in your life? Do you think that he may be using it to get you preoccupied with the demonic world all over again?" His answer was yes. I encouraged Thomas to spend time reading God's Word and getting energized by God's Spirit instead of focusing on the demonic world as much. He agreed. ☀

Many Christians today do the same thing as Thomas. Because the world of the demonic is intriguing, mystical, and dangerous, they get overly intrigued with the powers of darkness. Don't make that mistake. Know just enough about demons to recognize their power, strategies, and tendencies, but don't be enamored with them. ⑬

I could tell you stories about the demonic that would curl your toes. But I won't. These encounters in my life helped me understand the reality of the demonic world. The reason that I don't want to share these stories with you is that I feel too many people spend too much time focusing on the powers of darkness. They end up sensationalizing these evil angels and making them an object of intrigue among Christians. The result? An unhealthy preoccupation with the demonic. ☀

This chapter's goal is to give you the 4-1-1 on demons. You will receive just enough information to help you in your fight against them, but not enough to make you want to become obsessed with their dark power. C. S. Lewis said, "There are two equal and opposite errors into which our race can fall about the devils. One is to disbelieve in their existence. The other is to believe, and to feel an excessive and unhealthy interest in them. They themselves are equally pleased by both errors."[2] ✵

WHO ARE DEMONS?

Demons are the angels that rebelled with Satan in a futile attempt to overthrow God. Their fate was sealed in the deal. As soon as they chose to join the devil's rebel troops they sealed their eternal fate. No demon will ever stop being evil. No demon will ever repent. No demon will be rescued from the lake of fire. They are fallen angels on a highway to hell who want to take as many with them as possible into the eternal flames that await them. ✵

One third of the angels in heaven rebelled with Lucifer. "His tail swept a third of the stars out of the sky and flung them to the earth" (Revelation 12:4). We know that there are at least tens of millions of angels from Revelation 5:11. So we can assume that there are millions and millions of demons as well. They are everywhere. They are organized. And they hate you as much as the devil does. ✵

They are invisible enemies. The Bible makes it clear in Ephesians 6:12 that "our struggle is not against flesh and blood, but against . . . the spiritual forces of evil in the heavenly realms." In other words, our problems in life don't stem from earthly relationships, they stem from spiritual realities. Each of us would be shocked if we could see the invisible enemies behind a lot of our arguments, disagreements, unforgiveness, and bitterness. Satan uses his demonic forces to manipulate relationships in ways we cannot fathom. ⬢

HOW DO THEY OPERATE?

It's easy to imagine demons as kind of spastic and out of control. We tend to view them as running here and there starting trouble and causing problems. Most Christians probably don't think of them as superorganized. But they are. The Bible describes them as "the rulers . . . the authorities . . . the powers . . . the spiritual forces of evil in the heavenly realms" (Ephesians 6:12). These words indicate a highly organized system of armylike proportions. Imagine these demons as privates, sergeants, captains, colonels, and generals. They are not running around like crazed spirits wreaking unholy havoc on earthlings haphazardly. They are exacting, organized, disciplined, and dangerous. ⬢

One passage where you see this is Matthew 12:25–28 when Jesus said,

Every kingdom divided against itself will be ruined, and every city or household divided against itself will not stand. If Satan drives out Satan, he is divided against himself. How then can his kingdom stand? And if I drive out demons by Beelzebub, by whom do your people drive them out? So then, they will be your judges. But if I drive out demons by the Spirit of God, then the kingdom of God has come upon you.

This is a way of saying that Satan's team is organized and on the same page. Some religious rulers were accusing Jesus of casting out demons by the power of Satan. Jesus' response was basically that Satan and his demonic kingdom are not divided but organized. They work together for the same cause, mission, and vision in a disciplined way. They are just as organized today in their battle for your brain. ✹

We know that at least some demons are territorial. Daniel refers to a powerful demon as "the prince of the Persian kingdom" in Daniel 10:13. This may have been a short-term appointment, but at this particular time in history, he was in charge of the Persian kingdom. This indicates that all demons may be somewhat territorial, but we don't know that for sure. It's only a guess. ✹

WHAT DO THEY DO?

Demons are busy. They never sleep. They work around the clock to accomplish their mission of making Satan look good and God look bad. How do they do that? Primarily through trickery and deceit. They are masters of deception. A run of the mill demon could make the best magician in the world look like a second grader doing the severed thumb trick. ✹

Here are just a few of the wicked things they do.

THEY TRICK A FEW CHRISTIANS INTO ACCEPTING FALSE DOCTRINE

Demons want you bad. They want to deceive, distract, and, ultimately, destroy you. The Bible makes it clear that in the last days, "some will abandon the faith and follow deceiving spirits and things taught by demons" (1 Timothy 4:1). They want you to buy the lie. Maybe that lie has to do with who Jesus is, or how you enter into a relationship with God, or how you grow in your relationship with Christ, or how reliable the Bible is, or whatever. They want your brain. **◉**

Second Corinthians 10:3–5 describes this battle for your brain in stark military terms. **◉**

F *or though we live in the world, we do not wage war as the world does. The weapons we fight with are not the weapons of the world. On the contrary, they have divine power to demolish strongholds. We demolish arguments and every pretension that sets itself up against the knowledge of God, and we take captive every thought to make it obedient to Christ.*

The picture here is that your mind is locked away in a huge fortress controlled by the devil. The fortress has giant stone walls that seem impossible to scale, a huge iron gate that seems impossible to break, and a gigantic moat that seems impossible to cross. But armed with the Spirit of God and the ramrod of God's Word, you are called to charge full speed ahead and break through the walls to regain control of your mind from Satan and his demonic forces. Every time you memorize a verse, every time you pray, every time you crack open God's Word to study it, you are breaking open the fortress and regaining control of your brain thought by thought. **◉**

Now you may be thinking, *I've never lost control of my mind.* Oh, yes, you have. You and I were born with a fortress built by Satan around our minds. We were born in sin, and our thoughts make Satan smile. When you were born again (spiritually) you received Christ in your heart and received all the tools to develop a thought life that pleases God. But it takes work. It's a bloody battle for the "renewing of your mind" (Romans 12:2), which has been programmed through MTV, DVDs, secularism, your friends, and the world for most of your life. Ⓓ

Our goal should be to say with Paul, "But we have the mind of Christ" (1 Corinthians 2:16). This is when we have reached the point in our spiritual walk that God has control of the fortress of our thought patterns. This is when our first inclinations are to serve God. This is when our minds are so full of God's Word that we think like Jesus more often than not . . . and when we encounter a random thought that dishonors God we "take [it] captive . . . to make it obedient to Christ" (2 Corinthians 10:5). Ⓑ

THEY TEMPT ALL HUMANS WITH SIN

The devil tempted Jesus. You can be sure that his demons are tempting us. They dangle the pleasures of sin in front of us and whisper in our ears for us to give in and try the forbidden fruit. Ⓑ

Think of demons as evil fishermen. They bait their hooks with pleasure and lure their prey with fun so they can hook us with the consequences of sin. Their goal is to have us dangling off the riverbank on a string of fish ready for the frying pan. Ⓑ

Maybe for you that bait is sex. These master fishermen know how to use the surge of your adolescent hormones and the visually stimulating image of an incredible hunk or babe to get you to bite. ✪

Maybe that bait is cheating. The lure of good grades in an instant without the bother of studying dangles out there like a juicy fly to a hungry fish. ✪

Maybe that bait is anorexia. A quick fix to a perceived weight problem hooks many teenage girls in this society that idolizes the perfect body. ✪

I've done enough fishing to know that you bait the hook differently for different kinds of fish. Satan's army does the same thing to us. They are master fishermen who have a bait tailor-made for you. ✪

THEY TERRORIZE SOME
UNBELIEVERS THROUGH POSSESSION

Demons still possess people. I personally believe that the reason possession seemed more prevalent in Jesus' time is that Jesus had a way of drawing the demonic activity out. ✪

If a demon is "exorcised" out of somebody without that person ever putting his faith and trust in Christ as his Savior, "then it goes and takes seven other spirits more wicked than itself . . . and the final condition of that man is worse than the first" (Luke 11:26). ✪

DEMONS DO A WHOLE LOT MORE

"It is in the power of demons to cause dumbness (Matthew 9:32–33), blindness (Matthew 12:22), insanity

(Luke 8:26–35), personal injuries (Mark 9:18) . . . and to inflict suffering and deformities (Luke 13:11–17)."[3] ⬤

Not every physical illness is caused by the devil (John 9:1–3). We don't know how many illnesses are demon initiated. It could be a lot. It could be a few. But we know that some diseases and deformities are initiated by the forces of darkness. ⬤

The bottom line is that demons love to destroy. They would love to kill us, and they enjoy seeing families break apart and people fall apart. Like good fishermen they want another trophy to hang on their wall at the end of the day. Make sure it's not you. ⬤

HOW DO WE WIN AGAINST THEM?

Winning against demons doesn't come from some hocus pocus magic prayer. It doesn't come from chanting some phrase over and over again. It doesn't come from "claiming the blood of Jesus" over a house or a person. It comes from staying in the Word, staying close to Jesus, and staying away from sin. ⬤

When we stay close to Jesus we are, as Ephesians 6:10 calls us to be, "strong in the Lord and in his mighty power." This means that we are consistently cultivating our relationship with Jesus as our best friend. We are talking to the Father through prayer. We are depending on the Spirit through faith. We are not trying to take on the forces of evil in our own strength but in God's. ⬤

When we stay in the Word we are battering the fortress that surrounds our minds and claiming our brains and thoughts for Jesus Christ. We are establishing new strongholds that will keep demons out and right thoughts in. ⬡

When we stay away from sin we are not giving demons a way into our lives. The Bible calls us to avoid sin so that we "do not give the devil a foothold" (Ephesians 4:27). He and his posse can't pin us with sin because we are living in victory over sin. That doesn't mean that we never sin. But when we do we confess that sin to God and keep a clean slate before Him. Demons have no way in without sin. ⬡

A FINAL THOUGHT

Demons are real. Although we cannot see them, we can see the aftermath of their sinister strategies all around us. From suicide and murder to riots and racism, the results of their efforts splash across our newspaper headlines. ⬡

But the stories and statistics you don't hear much about are the ones that concern me the most. Two out of three high school teens currently going to church plan on leaving after they graduate from high school.[4] It is a premeditated graduation evacuation. And the forces of hell are rejoicing. ⬡

I'm convinced that the reason there is such fallout among Christian teens is that most never really owned their faith. Most have been borrowing it from their parents until the tassel is moved. Then the temptations that come with the college life or the "on your own" life after high school kick in. For these Christian teens the temptations are too great for their weak faith to overcome. ✪

When Christian teens graduate from high school, demons go on a feeding frenzy. Like vampires when the sun goes down, demons come out the night of graduation and, more often than not, they get their prey. ✪

Don't be lunch. ✪

PLATOON CHALLENGE

Have everybody break up into groups and answer these three questions, then come back together and send one representative from each group up front to share the answers from the group:

1. If we were demons, how would we attack this youth group?

2. What can we do as a group to prevent demons from destroying our group?

3. What don't we do enough of in our battle against demons and why?

AN ARMY OF ONE

1. How have you underestimated the presence and power of the forces of darkness in your own life?

2. How have you underestimated the presence and power of the Holy Spirit in your own life?

3. What will you do to stop underestimating?

6

TOUCHED BY AN ANGEL

"Do not forget to entertain strangers, for by so doing some people have entertained angels without knowing it."

HEBREWS 13:2

ngels want to help you. Demons want to hurt you. No surprise there. The shocking part comes when you begin to understand how powerful and intense the angels of God are. Too many times we picture angels as chubby cherubs that float around on clouds and are harmless as gnats. But the real story is different. Angels are awesome . . . and they are on your side, because you are on God's side. Think of them kind of like an army of cosmic big brothers that come to your aid when the demonic bullies start pushing you around. But get ready to have your stereotypes of angels blown away. And get ready to be touched by an angel, not the syrupy sweet ones on television, but the amazing ones in God's Word. ✹

According to Ron Rhodes, "The Bible has a lot to say about angels. The New Testament speaks of them some 165 times; the Old Testament, just over 100 times. Of course, even if the Bible mentioned angels just once, that would be enough for us to accept the doctrine as true."[1] ✹

Angels are all over the place in the Bible. They are carrying out God's commands, encouraging believers, pouring out God's judgments, and delivering messages. Angels are busy beings. They never sleep. They are not distracted by relationships. They have one focus, and that is to do what God says, when God says, how God says. ✹

A POPULAR MYTH

Many believe that when we as Christians die and go to heaven that we somehow magically transform into angels. They think that we sprout wings and hang out with a harp on a cloud. No. Angels are an entirely different kind of being. They are not human (although they sometimes pass as human when they go on "undercover" work for God on earth; e.g., Genesis 19:1–22). They never were human. We will never turn into angels ourselves. ●

A DIFFERENT BEING

Angels were created before humans were to carry out God's purposes in heaven and throughout this universe. When God was rebuking Job He said, "Where were you when I laid the earth's foundation? Tell me, if you understand. Who marked off its dimensions? Surely you know! Who stretched a measuring line across it? On what were its footings set, or who laid its cornerstone—*while the morning stars sang together and all the angels shouted for joy?*" (Job 38:4–7, italics added). This tells us that the angels were cheering God on as He created the universe. Like spectators at a heavenly Super Bowl, they yelled and applauded every time God scored another creation. They were His celestial cheerleaders as He created the cosmos and made this planet. ●

WHAT ARE ANGELS LIKE?

There are different types of angels that carry out God's commands. But all angels have a few things in common. Their main goal is to glorify God. Everything they do centers around pleasing Him. When Jesus prayed "your will be done on earth as it is in heaven," He was talking about how angels obey God immediately, completely, and wholeheartedly. Angels never argue with God; they obey Him. In that sense angels are a great example for us to follow. We should make it our goal to be as sold-out to glorifying God as the angels are. ✦

Angels glorify God by obeying Him without question when He tells them to do something. But they glorify Him in another way as well . . . through their worship. The angels are always singing and praising God. That is what they love and long to do. "Praise him, all his angels, praise him, all his heavenly hosts. . . . Let them praise the name of the Lord, for he commanded and they were created" (Psalm 148:2, 5). Again, this is something we can learn from the angels. We, too, were made to praise Him. God calls us to "sing and make music in your heart to the Lord, always giving thanks to God the Father for everything, in the name of our Lord Jesus Christ" (Ephesians 5:19–20). You were made for praise. So do you, like the angels, long and love to sing praises to Him? ✦

The word *angel* means "messenger." Angels are messengers between the heavenly and earthly realm. They sometimes bring good news (like in Luke 2:8–15 when the shepherds heard the word that the Messiah had been born in Bethlehem). Sometimes they bring bad news (like in Genesis 19 when they brought the news to Lot that the city he was living in was about to be destroyed by God). Sometimes their messages come in the form of action and not words. When the angels in the book of Revelation pour out God's wrath on this sinful planet, their actions speak louder than any words could. The message? "God is furious . . . repent!" ✹

WHAT DO ANGELS LOOK LIKE?

Angels are spirit beings, which means that they are normally invisible to the human eye. But when they do appear they don't all look the same. Some have wings and some don't. Some seem to look like men and some do not. Sometimes they appear as superhuman, and other times you couldn't tell them apart from a guy on the street (when they are on undercover work for God). But generally speaking, when an angel shows up, people run for cover in sheer terror. Oftentimes their first words to humans are "fear not." Why? Because they can be blindingly bright and look overwhelmingly powerful. Just in the first two chapters of the book of Luke there are three different appearances of angels to people, and each time their sudden appearance produced sheer terror in people's hearts. Every time these angels had to calm human fears by saying, "Do not be afraid." ✹

Some categories of angels don't look human at all. As a matter of fact they are somewhat beyond human description. Listen to the way the apostle John tries to describe some who surround the throne of God. ✹

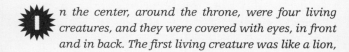

n the center, around the throne, were four living creatures, and they were covered with eyes, in front and in back. The first living creature was like a lion,

*the second was like an ox, the third had a face like a man,
the fourth was like a flying eagle. Each of the four living
creatures had six wings and was covered with eyes all
around, even under his wings. Day and night they never
stop saying, "Holy, holy, holy is the Lord God Almighty, who
was, and is, and is to come." (Revelation 4:6–8)*

These winged creatures (which we'll talk more about
later on) have one purpose . . . to lead all of heaven in a
continual chorus of praise to God. At their cue all of the
twenty-four elders who will surround the throne of God
in the future drop to their faces and cast their crowns at
the feet of Jesus. This symbolic act of worship happens
consistently throughout all of eternity. ✺

Personally, I believe that when these angels sing out
and the elders drop to their stomachs, it will be a worship
cue for all of heaven to face the throne of God and do the
same. These angels lead the way for praise in heaven.
They are so unique from the other angels that they are
called "creatures." Maybe each one represents a different
aspect of God's character. They have six wings and are
completely covered in eyes, perhaps to represent the fact
that God sees everything all the time; there is nothing
that escapes His notice. But in any case these angels are
awesome. ✺

HOW STRONG ARE ANGELS?

Angels are amazingly powerful. A very descriptive
passage of Scripture gives an insight into how strong
angels are. It takes place at the tomb of Christ when He

rose from the dead. "There was a violent earthquake, for an angel of the Lord came down from heaven and, going to the tomb, rolled back the stone and sat on it. His appearance was like lightning, and his clothes were white as snow. The guards were so afraid that they shook and became like dead men" (Matthew 28:2–4). This angel's mere presence caused a powerful earthquake. He descended from heaven and flicked the stone that was covering the entrance of Christ's tomb away like a pebble. This huge stone could have weighed as much as eight thousand pounds, according to some scholars.[2] In any case, this angel was so awesome, powerful, and intimidating that the big tough Roman soldiers who were guarding the tomb started convulsing in sheer terror and passed out. ✛

We know from Scripture that one angel, being used by God as an executor of justice upon Israel, killed 70,000 people in three days. We also know that in one night one angel killed 185,000 Assyrian warriors. We are no match for the angels of God. They are way more powerful than any of us. ✛

HOW MANY ANGELS ARE THERE?

Only heaven knows the answer to this question. But we do know from Revelation that when the apostle John caught a glimpse of heaven in the future, he "heard the voice of many angels, numbering thousands upon thousands, and ten thousand times ten thousand. They encircled the throne [of God]" (Revelation 5:11). Although this number is not exact, it does tell us that there are at least tens of millions (10,000 x 10,000 = 100,000,000).

Some have ventured a guess as to the exact number, but only heaven knows. ✴

WHAT DO ANGELS DO?

Angels carry out God's commands. A revealing picture of angels is tucked away in an obscure Old Testament passage, Genesis 28. Jacob had a dream, and in that dream he saw "a stairway resting on the earth, with its top reaching to heaven, and the angels of God were ascending and descending on it" (v. 12). God gave Jacob a glimpse into the everyday life of the typical angel. They would spend time traveling from heaven to earth to carry out a directive of God. When their mission was complete, they would make their way back up "the stairway to heaven" to get another mission to complete. This passage shows that the angels are active on earth and active in heaven. ✴

What do they do while on earth? All sorts of missions. Here is just a sampling from the Bible. God uses angels to:

- Deliver important messages (Daniel 10:4–14)

- Destroy sinners (Isaiah 37:36)

- Serve the saints (Hebrews 1:14)

- Minister to the needy (1 Kings 19:3–5)

- Help the helpless (Acts 12:6–11)

- Protect God's children (Matthew 18:10)

It seems from Matthew 18:10 that each of us may have a guardian angel who watches out for us individually. Jesus said, "See that you do not look down on one of these little ones. For I tell you that their angels in heaven always see the face of my Father in heaven." It seems like what Jesus is saying is that those with childlike faith in Jesus have angels designated to serve and protect them. These angels continuously look at the face of the Father, waiting for Him to say "go and protect my child" or "go and minister to my servant." According to this passage guardian angels may not be a myth after all. ✹

DIFFERENT KINDS OF ANGELS

CHOSEN ANGELS

These are the angels that did not follow Satan into sin and rebellion. These are your "typical" angels who carry out God's commands and ascend and descend between earth and the presence of God. Sometimes called "the heavenly host," these beings are many, powerful, and busy. They cannot sin. They cannot die. They cannot help but praise God. ✹

FALLEN ANGELS

These are the angels who did follow Satan into sin and rebellion. They hate God and His kingdom, but they must play by the rules or suffer judgment from God (Luke 8:31). They cannot do good. They will be cast into hell forever someday. They cannot help but hate Christians and Christ. ✹

SERAPHIM

Their title means "burning ones." They are continuously blazing in the presence of God as they belt out His praises. They are on fire for God. We see them in action in Isaiah 6:1–7. They flutter around God's throne with two of their six wings. One set of wings they use to cover their faces to shield themselves from the blinding light of God's glory. With two of the wings they cover their feet (perhaps showing their unwillingness to dare tread on the holy ground of God's temple). Their chief purpose is to proclaim the holiness of God to all of heaven. ✦

CHERUBIM

These are the "bodyguards of God" in His throne room. "The cherubim title speaks of their high and holy position and their responsibility as such is closely related to the throne of God as defenders of His holy character and presence."[3] Satan himself was a cherub . . . he was the number one defender of God's throne before he fell into sin (Ezekiel 28:14). ✦

SPECIFIC ANGELS

MICHAEL THE ARCHANGEL

Michael is God's number one angel (that's what "archangel" means). He is God's go-to angel when things are on the line. It seems from this title that he is in charge of all other angels and has the largest amount of God-given authority allotted to any angel. ✦

But as powerful as Michael is, his strength pales in comparison to Satan's. Jude 9 gives us an insight into Satan's superior strength. "But even the archangel Michael, when he was disputing with the devil about the body of Moses, did not dare to bring a slanderous accusation against him, but said, 'The Lord rebuke you!'" Michael dared not raise his voice to Satan, let alone his hand. Michael was no match for the devil. ✲

His name means "Who is like God?" His name shows that, as impressive as Michael is, he is not even close to the majestic and amazing King of the universe. Everything about Michael points to God and gives credit to Him. Unlike Satan, Michael has no desire to promote his own name. His only passion is to glorify God. What an example to us! ✲

So the question I must ask is this, Are you more like Michael or Satan? If you are all about you, then you have more in common with the devil. But if you live and breathe to make God famous, then you are more like Michael. I want to be like Mike! How about you? ✲

GABRIEL

This powerful angel is a true messenger. He delivered key messages from God to Daniel, Zechariah, and the virgin Mary. Each of these important messages had something to do with the birth of Christ. "Out of all the angels in the universe, God entrusted to Gabriel alone the greatest messages that ever left the courts of heaven—including the message of Christ's approaching birth." [4] ✲

What kind of messenger are you? God has entrusted to us the greatest message ever in all of the universe to deliver to an unsaved, unreached world . . . the gospel of Jesus Christ. Are you faithfully delivering this good news to those who need it the most? Are you carrying out the quest that God has given you of reaching your friends with the greatest message of human history? Be like Gabe!

THE ANGEL OF THE LORD

There is a kind of celestial mystery that clouds the identity of the Angel of the Lord. But the gentle breeze of God's Spirit and God's Word can clear the fog and show you just who he is . . . Jesus Christ Himself! ✦

Before Jesus ever appeared on this earth as a human, He appeared several times as the Angel of the Lord. He never was an actual angel technically. But in the looser sense of the word *angel,* meaning "messenger," He was the one who delivered His message to His people personally. Although He appeared to be a real angel, He wasn't. He was God Himself. We know this is Jesus Himself from passages like these:

Then he reached out his hand and took the knife to slay his son. But the angel of the LORD called out to him from heaven, "Abraham! Abraham!" "Here I am," he replied. "Do not lay a hand on the boy," he said. "Do not do anything to him. Now I know that you fear God, because you have not withheld from me your son, your only son." (Genesis 22:10–12, emphasis added)

There the angel of the Lord appeared to him in flames of fire from within a bush . . . When the Lord saw that he had gone

*over to look, God called to him from within the bush,
"Moses! Moses!" And Moses said, "Here I am!" "Do not come
any closer," God said. "Take off your sandals, for the place
where you are standing is holy ground." Then he said, "I am
the God of your father, the God of Abraham, the God of Isaac
and the God of Jacob." At this, Moses hid his face, because
he was afraid to look at God. (Exodus 3:2, 4–6)*

There are many other Old Testament passages that
show that the Angel of the Lord was Jesus Christ Himself.
This shows us that Jesus couldn't keep Himself away
from humanity. He is a God who longs to be connected
with His creation. He is a God who longs to be connected
with you! ☉

ARE ANGELS ACTIVE TODAY?

Are angels still ascending and descending on the stairway to heaven? Yes. Hebrews 13:2 makes it clear that we
should "not forget to entertain strangers, for by so doing
some people have entertained angels without knowing it."
Angels are among us doing undercover work for God.
Chances are you will never know who these "strangers"
are. But know this: They are on a mission from God, they
are on your side, and they are a powerful force. ☉

Remember that these angels are here to aid you in the
"battle zone" of life. They are God's reinforcements to
protect you, serve you, and encourage you in this war
against Satan. When the prophet Elisha and his servant
were surrounded by the Aramean army, Elisha's servant
freaked. ☉

When the servant of the man of God got up and went out early the next morning, an army with horses and chariots had surrounded the city. "Oh, my lord, what shall we do?" the servant asked. "Don't be afraid," the prophet answered. "Those who are with us are more than those who are with them." And Elisha prayed, "O LORD, open his eyes so he may see." Then the LORD opened the servant's eyes, and he looked and saw the hills full of horses and chariots of fire all around Elisha. (2 Kings 6:15–17)

God's angels, horses, and blazing chariots were standing between the enemy and Elisha. If we could open our eyes to the spiritual realm, we would be shocked at the intimidating demonic army that surrounds us, and we would be pumped by the angelic army that stands between us and them. They may be the "hedge" that surrounds us in between the spiritual battles that rage in our lives. ✹

All of us have heard stories of angel encounters. Some are made-up fables from freaked-out people. Others may be true. But whatever angel story you may hear, measure it by God's Word. If the so-called angel is delivering a message that contradicts God's Word, then you can be sure that the story is fake or the angel is fallen. Don't get caught up in all the celestial hype. Get caught up in what every good angel is caught up with . . . God Himself! ✹

PLATOON CHALLENGE

Break up into groups and draw two pictures (yes, complete with crayons, markers, etc.). Draw one picture of how angels are perceived in society and the other picture of how God describes them. Then do a show and tell with the whole group. (Insert elementary school flashback here.)

AN ARMY OF ONE

1. Ask yourself, "Am I more like Michael the archangel or Satan?" (In other words, do you draw attention to God or to yourself?)

2. Ask yourself, "Am I like Gabriel?" (In other words, are you faithful to deliver this all-important message of the gospel to those God has called you to?)

7

TEN MYTHS ABOUT SATAN AND SPIRITUAL WARFARE

"While we must give the devil his due, we dare not overestimate his power and province."[1]

HANK HANEGRAAFF

There are a lot of fables when it comes to the devil. Some of them come from tradition. From generation to generation stories have been told about the devil. As a result some of our perspective of Satan is more like the *National Enquirer* than the Bible.

Some of our perspective of the devil comes from movies like *The Exorcist* or *Lord of the Rings*. We picture the king of evil as something big, dark, horned, and flexed. We picture his demons running around like little madmen possessing everything in sight.

The problem is this: Whenever past myths or current culture has more of an impact than Scripture on our view of Satan, then we can be sure that our perspective is warped. And that's exactly what Satan wants you to have: a twisted perspective of him and his evil forces. If the devil can convince you that he is just a caricature rather than a real, powerful, and dangerous person, he has already got you beat.

So let's take a look at the top ten myths that are floating out there about the devil, demons, their power, and their plans. One by one I'm going to debunk these myths using God's Word. So let's start with the biggest myth.

MYTH 1:
THE DEVIL HAS HORNS, HOOVES, A TAIL, AND A PITCHFORK.

If I were to ask you to draw a picture of the devil, chances are your picture would contain horns, hooves, a tail, and a pitchfork. For centuries the devil has been painted like this. But this cartoon devil is far from reality. ⬟

If you remember from the first chapter, Satan was the most beautiful creation of God. God reminded Satan in Ezekiel 28:12 that "you were . . . perfect in beauty." There was no flaw in the devil. He was something to behold. He was drop-dead gorgeous. And there is no indication in the Bible that he changed his look after the Fall. As a matter of fact, he picked the most beautiful creature in the garden to represent him when he tempted Adam and Eve. ⬟

The bottom line is that we don't know what the devil looks like. No person on earth knows. But we do know this . . . he is not an ugly cartoon. He is real. He is beautiful. He is dangerous. ⬟

MYTH 2:
SATAN IS NOT REAL; HE WAS MADE UP TO EXPLAIN EVIL.

A lot of people believe that the devil is not real. They believe that he was made up to explain why we have evil in the world. Oftentimes the people who believe this have college degrees and spend time philosophizing and rationalizing the world in terms of what they can see. Anything they can't see, test, and prove is immediately rejected as false. These same people often view those who are spiritually inclined as naive, gullible, and uneducated. ●

The problem with this is that the Bible speaks of the devil as someone who is dangerously real. Satan is referred to as a "he" not an "it." He is described as a powerful, personal being with imposing intelligence. There is no indication in Scripture that the Prince of Darkness is a made-up myth. ●

From the third chapter of the Bible until the last chapter of the Bible, Satan is referred to hundreds of times as a reality. So, if Satan is just a made-up myth, then so is all of the Bible. ●

MYTH 3:
DEMON POSSESSION DOESN'T REALLY EVER HAPPEN TODAY.

What is demon possession? It's when a demon inhabits a person and takes complete control of him or her. Demonic manifestations were a regular occurrence throughout the New Testament, especially when Jesus walked the earth. Thomas Ice and Robert Dean Jr. give a great explanation as to why they seemed to be more active during the time of Jesus than now. ●

In parts of Texas during the summer you can look out at a field of Johnson grass and everything appears to be calm and inactive. However, when you walk through that field you stir things up. Often a wave of grasshoppers and other insects spring into action as you plod through the field. . . .The same was true of Christ's ministry. Often it was just his presence passing through the land of Israel that caused the activity of the demonic realm to become noticeable. The activity was there all along, but our Lord's messianic presence stirred up the spiritual realm and brought that activity out into the open.[1]

What does this mean? It means that Satan and his posse are just as active today as they were then. But their activities, especially when it comes to demonic possession, are more hidden and less obvious (in America anyway). ⊗

I have had my own demonic encounters. It's not something that I like to talk about. I think a lot of preachers sensationalize these situations and, oftentimes, unwittingly give glory to the devil. They tell descriptive stories of demonic possession or oppression and, inevitably, end up being the hero as they cast the evil demon into the abyss. To be honest I think the devil and his crew are not intimidated in the least by these kinds of preachers. I think they think many of them are a joke. Some of them are unknowingly in the devil's service, peddling a theology of magic formulas that will dispel the devil. ⓑ

Having established that there are a lot of wackos out there when it comes to dealing with the devil, I want to reaffirm this: I have had demonic encounters, and, chances are, so have you. We deal with the demonic every day. He uses his crew to tempt us and deceive us. And, when it comes to possession, chances are that you have encountered or will encounter someone who is possessed with a demon. The person may not be frothing at the mouth or levitating five feet off the ground, but in the inner caverns of his heart and soul the strings are being pulled by a fallen angel. ✿

Go to Africa and you will see a lot more "obvious" possessions. You have probably watched some National Geographic special showing a tribal warrior or witch doctor, eyes rolled back in his head, speaking what seems to be gibberish and gyrating uncontrollably. ✿

Personally, I believe that demonic possessions here in America are much less likely to be this kind. In my opinion the reason is that demons understand that a lot of people in America don't believe in possession. To turn up the heat and launch a frontal assault of head-twisting, puke-spewing, body-floating demonic possessions in America could back-fire and cause the intellectual elite to start believing in the unseen reality of demonic beings. To accept their existence is one step away from accepting the possibility of a Creator. That's why I believe demonic possession in America, while a reality, is far less obvious than in places like Africa. Satan is smart. ✿

MYTH 4:
DEMONS CAN POSSESS CHRISTIANS.

There are a lot of different opinions out there when it comes to whether or not a Christian can be demon possessed. Great men and women of God differ on this subject.

But after studying the Bible on this issue I became absolutely convinced that a true believer in Jesus Christ could never
be possessed by a demon. Here are a couple of reasons that
I believe this so strongly. First, there is no example in the
New Testament of a believer in Jesus Christ being demon
possessed. There are instances where Satan is influencing
believers or oppressing believers, but no examples of demons
possessing Christians. ✹

Second, for a demon to take possession of a Christian
he would have to first overthrow the Spirit of Jesus
guarding the soul of the Christian. The Bible makes it clear
in Ephesians 1:13–14 that "you also were included in
Christ when you heard the word of truth, the gospel of
your salvation. Having believed, you were marked in him
with a seal, the promised Holy Spirit, who is a deposit
guaranteeing our inheritance until the redemption of
those who are God's possession—to the praise of his
glory." That means that as soon as we trust in Jesus Christ
as our Savior, the Lord causes His Holy Spirit to live inside
us. He is commissioned by God to stay inside us until we
are in the very presence of God Himself in heaven. He
lives inside us as proof to us that we are His. And the
Holy Spirit is God's down payment on our soul. He is there
to strengthen us to serve God, set us apart from sin,
encourage us when we are discouraged, and protect our
souls from evil. ✹

When the Spirit of God seals the soul of the believer it
is almost as though He puts a "do not disturb" sign on the
heart of the believer. No demon can enter when that sign
is on. And it's always on. ✹

For a demon to take possession of the soul of a believer, he has to face the Spirit of Jesus head on. Here's how Jesus put it in Luke 11:21–22, "When a strong man, fully armed, guards his own house, his possessions are safe. But when someone stronger attacks and overpowers him, he takes away the armor in which the man trusted and divides up the spoils." ✷

What Jesus is saying is that when a demon possesses a man or a woman, the demon is the strongman who is in control of that soul. The demon is going to control and protect his turf. When Jesus comes into someone's life, He becomes "the soul stealer." He takes the demon, ties him up, throws him out, and steals that soul for God. ✷

How does this prove that a Christian could never be possessed by a demon? Simple: When a demon possesses a soul, that person's only hope is that Jesus comes in and takes control of that soul. Then He becomes the strongman. He becomes the "bodyguard." Now that soul is His turf. So for a demon to take possession of that soul again, he would first have to tie up Jesus and throw Him out. That's not going to happen. ✷

Before I got into the ministry I was a roofer. I had a friend named Art who I used to work with every day. He had just gotten out of the army and was bulging with muscles. He was six feet one inch tall, weighed about 195 pounds, and had about 5 percent body fat. He could bench-press more than three hundred pounds and was as tough as nails. ✷

One day when we went to work we encountered a serious problem. The roof we had been working on the day before had other roofers on it. We had spent all day the day before preparing the roof, flashing in the skylights, and preparing one entire side for the roofing material to be put on. Somehow another crew came to our jobsite and jumped on the side of the roof that we had spent all day the day before preparing. The problem was that we got paid by how much roofing material we put down, and the guys had "stolen" our side of the roof. As we drove closer to the jobsite we could see the guys on our side, and Art began ranting that he was going to beat them both up. I tried to calm him down by saying, "Art, let me handle it." ☀

I'll never forget getting out of the truck right under that side of the roof and starting a conversation that went something like this:

"Nice day, isn't it, guys?"

"Yeah, it's great," one of the roofers said.

"You know that yesterday we came out and spent the entire day prepping this side of the roof," I said with a smile.

"So what?" he responded.

"Well, I don't really think it's fair that we spend an entire day preparing this side of the roof and you guys come this morning and take it from us. That's money out of our pockets. By rights that side of the roof is our turf," I said, still smiling.

"Well, it's a big house; why don't you just jump on another side?" he retorted with a few expletives mixed in.

Now all of this time Art was just standing there heaving in a sleeveless shirt. His biceps were flexed, his brow furrowed, and his eyes burning with anger. So I said, "Guys, I totally understand. But my friend here, he just doesn't get it. As a matter of fact, it was all I could do to convince him to let me talk to you first this morning as we pulled up. You see, he wants to tear you limb from limb and then throw you physically from this roof. But I don't want it to come to that. I just want to convince you to pick another side yourself so that we all can have a great day." ✸

When those two guys looked at the size of Art and the crazed look in his eyes, they almost ran to the other side of the roof. You see, I had somebody a lot bigger than me protecting my turf. And when those guys saw him, they ran. ✸

You have somebody bigger and badder than Art protecting the "turf" of your soul. His name is Jesus Christ. When demons see the size of His biceps, they run. There is no way they would even try to steal your soul, because to do that they would have to take out Jesus. Not going to happen. ✸

MYTH 5:
DEMONS CAN'T HURT
CHRISTIANS AT ALL.

Now although a demon could never possess a Christian, demons can attack us in other ways. How? ✸

First of all, demons can tempt Christians to sin. Although Satan and his demonic army's power were crushed at the cross, they still have the power of the whisper and the power of the roar. Ⓑ

THE POWER OF THE WHISPER

At some point in your cartoon-watching career, you probably have seen some poor character with a little demon on one shoulder and a little angel on the other. The little cartoon demon whispers into the ears of his victim why he should and the little angel whispers in the other ear why he shouldn't. Well, this is not too far from the truth. Satan's power was totally obliterated at the cross. But he and his posse still have the power of the whisper. They whisper in our ears things like:

- "Nobody will know if you and your boyfriend have sex."

- "It's OK as long as you both really love each other."

- "Everybody surfs these kinds of sites."

- "Cheating is not a real sin. It's not like you're stealing a car or something."

- "Go ahead; it's just a little white lie."

The power of a whisper is amazing. As a professional speaker, I get pretty intense. When I am on a roll in front of a crowd, my veins pop out, sweat pours out of my body, and my arms flail in every direction. I hate to admit it, but I am a spastic preacher. ❂

But if I really want to get a crowd's attention I whisper. Right in the middle of a lightning-fast, high-impact aerobics, arm-flailing talk, if I throw in a whisper the crowd of teenagers almost leans forward to hear what I am saying. That's what Satan does to us. In the middle of our fast-paced, loud days he whispers his lies in our ears and, too often, we listen and obey. ⓑ

THE POWER OF THE ROAR

Satan is called "a roaring lion" in 1 Peter 5:8. There is something interesting about roaring lions on the African plains. Most of the male lions that roar are not the primary hunters. It's the female lions in the pride that usually stalk and kill the prey. These lionesses usually hunt at dusk and into the night. They stalk their prey by hiding in the brush and the bushes waiting for one of the animals to stray too far from the safety of the herd. Then the lionesses surge and seize their prey in a short burst of power and fury. Once the prey is killed, that's when the older male lions join the feast on the carcass of the zebra, antelope, water buffalo, or other animal. ◉

The roars of these male lions can be heard up to five miles away and can be quite intimidating. But the roaring lion is not usually the one that kills. It's the lionesses hiding in the bushes. In the same way Satan's roar cannot hurt us. But it can scare us. He is sending his "lionesses" of temptation and deception to hide in the bushes and wait for us to stray from the safety of the presence of Jesus. Once we do, these temptations jump from the brush and take us out . . . and Satan comes to enjoy the feast. What's the lesson? Don't be scared by the roar, and keep your eyes on the bushes. The roars of Satan, although loud and intimidating, cannot hurt us if we stay close to Jesus. It's the secret sins in the bushes that will take you down so that Satan can come and tear you limb from limb. ⚙

The roaring lion is sending some lionesses your way to stalk you and destroy you so that he can feast on your failure. Here are just a few of his stalking "lionesses" that are lurking behind the bushes with your destruction in mind. ⚙

HATRED

Somebody hurt you and you want to get back at him. That raging roar of hatred you feel in your heart is from the Evil One himself. Deadly hate is just waiting for you to give in so that she can seize your soul and Satan can have his lunch. ⚙

LUST

Those nasty thoughts that burn in your soul for that member of the opposite sex (or in some instances same sex) is the stalking lioness of lust. The roaring lion is just waiting for you to give in to that sin. If you surge to that urge, then the jaws and claws of compromise will sink deeply into your soul. ⚙

GOSSIP

That story that you want to tell about somebody else's dark secrets is screaming to get out. Share it and you are are a fallen angel's appetizer. ⚙

So what should we do when we hear that roar? Keep your eyes on the brush and the bushes for the stalking sins that want to destroy you so that Satan can roar over your carcass. We should stand firm in the armor of God and fight him in the power of Jesus. Because when Jesus died on the cross, Satan was doomed to be declawed and defanged completely someday. Until then he is a roaring lion looking for someone like you to devour. **⬢**

MYTH 6:
THE DEVIL IS A WIMP.

Some people think the devil is a wuss. They are wrong. He is the biggest, strongest, smartest, and fiercest creation of God. As we talked about in chapter 1, Satan has no equal among all that God has made. **⬢**

There is a pretty blunt section of Scripture that tells us how we should view Satan:

n the very same way, these dreamers pollute their own bodies, reject authority and slander celestial beings. But even the archangel Michael, when he was disputing with the devil about the body of Moses, did not dare to bring a slanderous accusation against him, but said, "The Lord rebuke you!" Yet these men speak abusively against whatever they do not understand. (Jude 8–10)

Basically Jude is telling us that we shouldn't dis the devil for two main reasons:

- It's something stupid people do. **⬢**

Jude calls them "dreamers." In other words, they are living in their own little fantasy world. It is stupid to pick a fight with the devil. **⬢**

- It's something angels never do. **⬢**

The strongest angel of God, Michael, didn't dare try to take on Satan by himself. Why? Because Satan would beat him to a pulp in a fist fight. So if God's toughest angel couldn't beat the devil and wouldn't pick a fight with Satan, why would we? ⬦

Notice what Michael did when he had his showdown with the devil. He said, "The Lord rebuke you!" In other words, Michael ran to Jesus for help. He depended on the Lord to defeat Satan and not on himself. That's exactly what we should do. When the devil wants to throw down with us, we trust in God and ask Him to defeat this evil and powerful enemy. ⬦

MYTH 7:
SATAN AND HIS CREW RULE OVER HELL.

If you look at cartoons of the devil, often he and his demonic army are pictured ruling over hell, taunting and torturing lost sinners with their pitchforks. I don't know where this idea came from, but it is dead wrong. Maybe it came from a few obscure passages that refer to some demons who are in hell right now. ⬦

And the angels who did not keep their positions of authority but abandoned their own home—these he has kept in darkness, bound with everlasting chains for judgment on the great Day. (Jude 6)

. . . God did not spare angels when they sinned, but sent them to hell, putting them into gloomy dungeons to be held for judgment . . . (2 Peter 2:4)

It seems that there were a group of angels that rebelled with Satan and at some point did something so evil, so unheard of, that God put them into hell earlier than the other demons. As a matter of fact, they are there right now even as you read these words. They are not ruling over hell. Hell is ruling over them. They are in a dark dungeon, locked in chains waiting for the Judgment Day. ✹

Here are two more reasons that we know Satan is not ruling over hell right now.

- The devil is operating in the atmosphere of earth, not the flames of hell. ✹

The Bible calls Satan "the ruler of the kingdom of the air" in Ephesians 2:2. He has the ability to zoom back and forth across this planet through the air and do his wicked deeds while accomplishing his twisted plan. When God asked Satan where he had been in Job 1, Satan responded by saying, "From roaming through the earth and going back and forth in it" (v. 7). Satan is on the loose on the earth, not ruling in hell. ✹

- Someday Satan and his followers will be cast into hell for good. ✹

The Bible talks about a day when Satan and all of his demonic followers will be cast into hell for good. "And the devil, who deceived them, was thrown into the lake of burning sulfur, where the beast and the false prophet had been thrown. They will be tormented day and night for ever and ever" (Revelation 20:10). When Satan is thrown into the lake of fire, he will be too busy burning to rule anything. More on this in the final chapter. ✹

MYTH 8:
IF I JUST REBUKE THE DEVIL, HE MUST STOP.

What is a rebuke? It is when somebody tries to stop the devil by just speaking out loud to Satan and saying something like "Satan, you have no place here. I bind you. I rebuke you. You must stop." But it takes more than just words to stop the devil, and Scripture never tells us to speak to the devil anyway. The Bible makes it crystal clear in James 4:7, "Submit yourselves, then, to God. Resist the devil, and he will flee from you." God gives us a strategy to stop the devil in his tracks. It is a two-part plan to defeat the devil in any and every temptation situation. ❽

It starts with submitting yourself to God. Before you can defeat the devil you need to make sure the Spirit of God is in control of your soul. When you face that temptation situation, take a moment and ask God to take the steering wheel. Surrender yourself fully to Him. Confess any sins that are blocking your relationship with the Lord, and let Him take full control. This gets you back in "the power zone." What is the power zone? It is when we are operating in God's strength and not our own. It is when the Spirit of God is calling the shots and not us. Ephesians 6:10 reminds us that getting in the power zone is the key to defeating the devil. "Finally, be strong in the Lord and in his mighty power." ❽

Trying to take the devil on in your own strength is like trying to beat the Incredible Hulk in an arm-wrestling match. Ain't gonna happen. But once you submit to the power of God, His strength surges through your soul and you become an unstoppable force of unbelievable power. ✿

The second part of the strategy to defeat your enemy is to "resist the devil." Now it's a lot easier to resist the devil once you are armored with the power of God. When you are operating in God's strength and not your own, you just say no to his roars and his whispers. You resist the temptation. You endure the trouble. You win against sin in the power of God. ✿

God's promise in this passage is that when we are empowered by God and say no to the devil, then he will run away. He knows that he can't win against us if we are living a life that is propelled by God's power. So he runs away. But don't worry, he'll be back another day, hoping that you are not living in the power zone. ✿

Defeating the devil doesn't start with a rebuke or shouting out, "Satan, I bind you in the name of Jesus!" It takes more than TV-preacher tricks. It takes more than magic words or simple formulas. It takes resisting the devil by unleashing the power of God surging through your soul. It takes a strong relationship with Jesus. ✿

MYTH 9:
SATAN ATTACKS ALL CHRISTIANS EQUALLY.

Satan doesn't attack all Christians equally. Think about it. If you were the devil, who would you spend your time attacking? Would you waste a lot of time on Christians who are discouraged by troubles or defeated by sin? Or would you focus your efforts on those who were living radical lives for God? The answer is obvious. ❂

About four hundred years ago a preacher named Richard Baxter said to fellow pastors, "Take heed to your-selves because the tempter will make his first and sharpest assault on you. If you will be leaders against him, he will not spare you. He bears the greatest malice against the man who is engaged in working the greatest damage against him."[2] In other words, the degree to which you are making a dent in Satan's kingdom is the degree to which he wants to make a dent in your head. ❂

Just go back to the book of Job and you will see this truth. Job was a man of God. He lived a life that honored the Lord, and that made the devil mad. As a result Satan got God's permission to unleash his full arsenal against Job to get him to compromise. Why? Because Job was doing the most damage to his evil kingdom. People were being impacted for the Lord by Job's example. One of Job's best friends, Eliphaz, acknowledged the impact Job had made for God's kingdom when he told Job, "Think how you have instructed many, how you have strengthened feeble hands. Your words have supported those who stumbled; you have strengthened faltering knees" (Job 4:3–4). In other words, Job was making a difference with his life. He helped others. He served others. He shared God's truth and God's love with every-body he encountered. So Satan wanted to stop him at all costs and as soon as possible. ❂

What does this mean for you? If you are living a life of sin and compromise you probably don't have to worry much about spiritual warfare. Why would Satan waste his limited time and efforts on you? But if you are living a life that affects others and honors God, watch out—Satan has you in his crosshairs. ⚙

MYTH 10:
TRUE SPIRITUAL WARFARE IS RARE.

When many Christians think of spiritual warfare, they think of some surreal kind of cartoon battle of good angel versus bad angel in the invisible spirit world. Others imagine some kind of *Buffy the Vampire Slayer* or *X-Files* adventure. Still others conjure up thoughts of movies like *The Exorcist*, where good meets bad in a battle for the body. As a result spiritual warfare seems rare. It seems like an X-Men adventure in the underworld underground. The result? Most Christian teens don't take it seriously. ⚙

That is a mistake. 🅑

The Bible says something very interesting about spiritual warfare. According to God's Word, this unseen battle takes place in the context of relationships and the brain. 🅑

Ephesians 6:12 shows us that this spiritual battle is in the middle of everyday relationships with people, "For our struggle is not against flesh and blood, but against the rulers, against the authorities, against the powers of this dark world and against the spiritual forces of evil in the heavenly realms." Those relationships that you are struggling with, that brother who keeps picking on you, those students at your school who are making fun of your Christianity, that teacher who verbally criticizes your belief system in class, all have an invisible reality behind them. You see, our problem is not with "flesh and blood." In other words, our problem is not with people. Our problem is with the devil, who uses those relationships to discourage, distract, and deceive us. Relationships are a battlefield for spiritual warfare . . . and so is your mind. ✿

Second Corinthians 10:4–5 make it clear that our brains are a battlefield. "The weapons we fight with are not the weapons of the world. On the contrary, they have divine power to demolish strongholds. We demolish arguments and every pretension that sets itself up against the knowledge of God, and we take captive every thought to make it obedient to Christ." These verses are filled with military terms. God tells us that we have powerful weapons to bust through satanic strongholds in our brains. What is a stronghold? It is a wall of wrong thinking that keeps God out. It is the moat around our minds that refuses to allow the Word of God to penetrate. It is the iron gate of sin, built by Satan himself to keep our thoughts worldly. ✿

When you became a Christian your soul was saved. You were adopted as a child of God and your sins were nailed to the cross. You became a new creation in Christ. You have a new Father, a new home in heaven, and a new path to walk. But you need a new mind as well. Satan has lost your heart to Jesus, and the last thing he wants is to lose your mind to Jesus. So he establishes strongholds (walls, moats, gates, etc.) of wrong thinking to keep your brain thinking wrong thoughts about God, life, relationships, movies, music, sin, and him. ✿

How do we break through these strongholds? We use our weapons. We use the catapult of God's Word and the ramrod of God's Spirit to break through the gates, shatter the walls, and recapture our thoughts for God. Your brain is a battlefield. ✸

MORE MYTHS

For every truth of God, Satan has an arsenal of lies. In other words, there are more than ten myths when it comes to the devil and spiritual warfare. What's a Christian teenager to do? Measure everything you hear by God's Word. New bank tellers are trained to spot counterfeit money, not by studying counterfeit money, but by becoming familiar with the real thing. The same is true of spiritual warfare. The way you identify Satan's lies is by becoming superfamiliar with God's truth. The more time you spend studying God's Word and depending on God's Spirit, the more you will be able to tell a counterfeit from the real thing. ✸

PLATOON CHALLENGE

1. Set up a debate with one side defending two specific myths and one side debunking those two myths. Be sure to use your Bibles.

2. Have a panel of judges pick which side won, and why.

AN ARMY OF ONE

Which of the myths did you buy into before reading this chapter? Circle your answers:

1. The devil has horns, hooves, a tail, and a pitchfork.

2. Satan is not real; he was made up to explain evil.

3. Demon possession doesn't really ever happen today.

4. Demons can possess Christians.

5. Demons can't hurt Christians at all.

6. The devil is a wimp.

7. Satan and his crew rule over hell.

8. If I just rebuke the devil, he must stop.

9. Satan attacks all Christians equally.

10. True spiritual warfare is rare.

HOW TO WIN THE WAR FOR THE SOULS OF YOUR FRIENDS

"At the core of leadership is one, single trait: belief in a cause."[1]

RICHARD MARCINKO, FORMER COMMANDER, U.S. NAVY

We are at war. We may not be able to see the bullets and bombs exploding around us, but it is happening nonetheless. Every day you go to school you are entering a battle zone. You are in a fight to the death with Satan for your friends who don't know Jesus Christ as their Savior. Satan will do everything in his immense power to get you to give up. But you must win. The stakes are too high for you to lose. What is at stake? The eternal souls of your friends!

Second Timothy 2:26 makes it clear that we need to pray for the lost "that they will come to their senses and escape from the trap of the devil, who has taken them captive to do his will."

So how do we rescue our friends who are prisoners of this diabolical enemy? There are five strategic actions that you must execute if you expect victory at the end of the day.

FACE THE GRIM REALITY

You must be brutally honest about your friends . . . they are POWs. Now I know a little about prisoners of war, because my dad was one. He was a master sergeant in the United States Army. He was captured by the North

Koreans, tortured for his faith in God and country, and kept as a prisoner for years. He was the *last* POW to be released from the war with the North Koreans. When he was finally released, there was a huge parade and celebration held in his honor. ✪

Your friends are prisoners of Satan's war against God. When they are finally rescued from his dungeon of sin, there will be a huge celebration in heaven in their honor! Jesus said in Luke 15:10, "There is rejoicing in the presence of the angels of God over one sinner who repents." Every time someone comes to Christ, there is a party in heaven. Why? Because the person has been set free from years as a POW and is now a citizen in the kingdom of God. ✪

Satan is described in Isaiah 14:17 as the one "who made the world a desert, who overthrew its cities and would not let his captives go home." But Jesus changed all of that. Isaiah later wrote that the coming Christ would "proclaim freedom for the captives and release from darkness for the prisoners" (61:1). That's what Jesus did. He set the captives free from the dungeon of sin and brought them into His very own family! ✪

What does all of this mean? It means that until your friends hear the gospel and believe, until they have an encounter with Jesus, they are chained by sin, tortured by Satan, and imprisoned in an endless cycle of futility. No wonder suicide is a leading cause of death among high schoolers! Apart from Christ there is no hope in the inner sanctuary of the teenaged soul. ✪

God wants to use you to free them. There is no plan B. ✪

INVADE THE ENEMY'S TERRITORY

The Bible describes us as "aliens and strangers on earth" in Hebrews 11:13. That means that this earth is not our real home. As soon as you trusted in Christ, heaven became your real home. This earth is enemy territory under Satan's command. ❂

Behind all the headlines, behind all the wars and rumblings, behind all the stories and stats of destruction and crime, there is an evil being pulling the strings . . . Satan himself. God has given him temporary command of planet Earth. The results you can read about every day in the newspaper. ❽

We as believers are called to invade this dangerous turf and rescue those who have been held captive by the devil. Make no mistake about it, this is no fairy tale or Hollywood story line. It is real. There is a real devil (who is dangerous), a real mission (which takes courage), and real victims (who need rescue). That's where you come in. Jesus' final words on this planet were "and you will be my witnesses in Jerusalem, and in all Judea and Samaria, and to the ends of the earth" (Acts 1:8). You are on a search-and-rescue mission behind enemy lines. ❽

Now you may be thinking, *I thought God ruled everything?* He does. As Hank Hanegraaff says again and again on his radio show, "There is not one renegade molecule in the universe." Ultimately everything and everyone is under His command. But just like God chose to give the rule of the planet to Adam in Genesis 1, He allowed Satan to wrestle control of this planet from Adam in Genesis 3. The earth is under Satan's control until Jesus comes back and claims it for His own. In the unseen world behind the world that you and I see with our eyes, there is another world, an invisible realm, where Satan calls the shots. Here are two clear verses from the Bible that describe Satan as the ruler of the world:

> **A**s for you, you were dead in your transgressions and sins, in which you used to live when you followed the ways of this world and of the ruler of the kingdom of the air, the spirit who is now at work in those who are disobedient. (Ephesians 2:1–2)

We know that we are children of God, and that the whole world is under the control of the evil one. (1 John 5:19)

This doesn't mean that Satan can do anything he wants anytime he wants. He still must give an account to God. There is nothing he can do without God's green light. It's like a football field. God draws the lines that Satan must "play" within. God always has His flag ready to throw to keep the devil in line. ✪

The point is this: Satan rules this planet temporarily, and when you invade his turf to steal souls from his kingdom, it makes him mad. He will do everything he can to stop you. He never sleeps and has only one thing on his mind . . . destroying God's plan and kingdom by crushing God's children through sin and compromise. ✪

THROW THE G-O-S-P-E-L GRENADE

It doesn't matter who throws a grenade, it's going to explode. It could be a seasoned army general, a young marine recruit, or a twelve-year-old girl. A grenade is an equal opportunity destroyer. ✪

In a lot of ways the gospel is like a grenade. It doesn't matter who gives it, there is going to be some kind of spiritual explosion in the unseen world. Paul wrote some intense stuff about this in Romans 1:16. "I am not ashamed of the gospel, because *it is the power of God* for the salvation of everyone who believes" (italics added). That word *power* means explosive power, because when people come to Christ they are blown out of the kingdom of darkness into the kingdom of God. The message of Christ is quite literally a blast. It doesn't matter who throws that holy grenade. It could be Billy Graham or a twelve-year-old girl, the results are still the same . . . explosive. ✺

So what is the gospel message? It is a story and a creed. It is the ultimate love story that begins in Genesis 1 and culminates in Revelation 22. From the first chapter of the Bible to the last it, is a blast. Here is that powerful message:

God created us to be with Him.

Our sins separate us from God.

Sins cannot be removed by good deeds.

Paying the price for sin, Jesus died and rose again.

Everyone who trusts in Him *alone* has eternal life.

Life that's eternal means we will be with Jesus forever in heaven.

Memorize it . . . word for word. Make sure you know it backward and forward. Be able to explain this story to your friend point by point. It's not hard—it's a love story that explodes. It will blast your friends out of the dungeon of Satan into the family of God. Pull the pin, chuck the bomb, then duck. ◉

GET READY FOR A FIERCE COUNTERATTACK

The more you try to steal souls from the devil's dungeon, the more you will be targeted by the Evil One. He gets ticked when you rescue prisoners of war. ◉

There are several ways that he will seek to stop you. His counterattacks vary with your personality type and spiritual and emotional weaknesses. He has seen our kind for thousands of years and is able to size us up pretty quickly. You can be sure he has a counterattack tailor-made for you. Here are just a few of his devilish strategies. ◉

HE WILL TRY TO DISTRACT YOU WITH TOYS

We live in a world of X-boxes, Gameboys, and Play Stations. We have CDs, DVDs, High Speed Internet, Blockbuster, and the mall. We can get access to hundreds of stations through the "dish" and thousands of songs through MP3s. It's not that these things are bad in and of themselves. But they can be toys of distraction to keep us from going to war. To sidetrack us from reaching our friends for Jesus Christ, Satan can keep us busy online, in front of the television, or just jamming in our room to our favorite songs. Think of Satan as an evil Santa Claus who wants to fill your stocking every day with fun stuff to keep you from the real war raging all around you. ✪

HE WILL TRY TO DECEIVE YOU WITH LIES

> "Just build the relationship a little longer."
>
> "You have plenty of time to reach your friend."
>
> "Just wait until they see something different about your life first."
>
> "If you witness to them, you could lose them as your friends forever."
>
> "What if they ask you a question that you can't answer?"

On and on Satan's arsenal of lies goes until he pounds you into silent submission. Jesus calls him "a liar and the father of lies" (John 8:44). He was the one who invented the concept. He lied to Eve. He lies to us. And he's good at being bad. He is a master deceiver who knows exactly how to trick us. Our only defense is the Spirit of God, the armor of God, and the Word of God. So get empowered, get dressed, and get studying. ✪

HE WILL TRY TO DISCOURAGE YOU WITH FAILURE

Think about the word *discourage*. It means to take your courage away. When you are discouraged, you aren't bold for Christ in the battle. When you are discouraged, the devil robs you of your boldness to live and give your faith. ✪

Satan wants to beat the courage out of you with failure. Whether it be bad grades at school, a relationship blunder, a sports "choke," or a job loss, Satan wants to beat you up and keep you down. He can use your discouragement to make your eyes turn inward instead of upward. His strategy is to so deflate you that you won't even think about reaching your friends for Jesus Christ. ✪

When I was in high school, there was a girl I really liked. The feelings were not mutual. I can remember being so discouraged because of the whole situation. It brought me down so much that Satan used it to get me focused on myself instead of rescuing souls from the devil's domain. ✪

Maybe you are involved in a relationship that is bringing you down, or maybe it's your situation at home. Perhaps your parents fight so much that you don't even want to be at home. Or maybe you have a friend who is stabbing you in the back, and it's bumming you out. ✪

Just remember, Satan wants to use those situations to discourage you, but God wants to use those trials to build you. God reminds us in James 1:2–4, "Consider it pure joy, my brothers, whenever you face trials of many kinds, because you know that the testing of your faith develops perseverance. Perseverance must finish its work so that you may be mature and complete, not lacking anything." In other words, God uses those troubles and trials to make you tough. ✪

Like a boot camp for the soul, trials make us tougher, tighter, and spiritually ripped . . . if we respond to them in faith. If not, they discourage us from the battlefront and make us retreat into our foxholes. Don't allow Satan to discourage you. ❽

HE WILL TRY TO DESTROY YOU WITH SIN

Sin is fun. If it wasn't, we wouldn't do it so much. There is something deeply satisfying about tearing a person down behind his back. There is an incomparable thrill in the rush of lust. We feel a sense of sneaky superiority when we pull the wool over somebody else's eyes. We love to fuel the fire of road rage when we are being tailgated by that "jerk" behind us. And on and on the list of naughtiness goes. ❾

The Bible is pretty blunt about the short-term happiness that sin can bring. Speaking of Moses God tells us, "He chose to be mistreated along with the people of God rather than to enjoy the pleasures of sin for a short time" (Hebrews 11:25). The KJV translation of the Bible says he chose not to enjoy sin's pleasures "for a season." Hot summer sin inevitably leads to cold winter frostbite. Satan will tempt us to give in to the sin and enjoy the short-term pleasures of it. But sooner or later God will have His due. ❿

Satan will use sin to destroy the power of our witness and rob us of the power of God. He will cut short our walk with God, make us wallow in the backwash of guilt, and try to keep us swirling in a downward spiral in the dirty toilet of debauchery. ⓫

DON'T LET SATAN GET YOU!

Watch out. Satan is a prowling lion, a lying snake, a destroying dragon, an angry angel. He wants to distract you with toys, deceive you with lies, discourage you with failure, and destroy you with sin. Every moment of every day he is plotting ways to bring you down. But through Christ's death on the cross and resurrection from the dead, and through His Holy Spirit who lives in you, the victory is already yours. ✸

DON'T GO INTO BATTLE ALONE

A Christian without church is like a soldier without an army . . . in trouble. When I mention the word *church,* you probably think about the place that you go with your parents every Sunday morning. And that's part of it. But "church" is a bigger concept than just a *place* of worship. Actually the word *church* means a group of people who believe the same thing and worship the same person. There are local churches (where we fellowship, worship, take communion, and learn from God's Word), and there is the "universal church." This is made up of all believers from all times and all over the world. When you meet somebody for the first time at school and realize that he or she is a Christian, then you are meeting someone who is part of the universal body of Christ. You are united with other believers in some mystical way as part of the same family. ✸

The bottom line is that we need each other. We are an army of God against the forces of darkness. All of us work together for the advancement of God's kingdom with the promise that the "gates of hell will not prevail" against us. Jesus painted the picture of the church as a battering ram against the gates of the devil's castle. They won't prevail. Sooner or later the bolts will bust, the wood will splinter, and we will win. ✪

Studying the structure of an army is pretty interesting. There are corps, divisions, brigades, regiments, battalions, companies, platoons, and squads. Generally a squad is a small group of soldiers who fight together in a team of seven or eight. It takes three or four squads to make up a platoon, four or five platoons to make up a company, three or four companies to make up a battalion, three or four battalions to make up a regiment, three regiments to make up a brigade, three brigades to make up a division, three divisions to make up a corps, and more than one corps to make up an army. ✪

Think of the universal church as an army, all the believers on the planet today as a corps. The other corps are in heaven waiting for us to join them. Think of all the churches in the United States as a division, in your state as a brigade, in your city as a regiment, and in your community as a battalion. Think of all the believers in your church as a company, in your youth group as a platoon, and in your "E-Team" as a squad. Now would probably be a good time to introduce you to the concept of the E-Team, which I'll describe in more detail a bit later. Like the early disciples, the E-Team sets the pace for effective outreach for the whole army, and specifically the battalions and platoons they are a part of. "E" stands for evangelism. ✪

Your E-Team squad is a handful of special forces soldiers who have a specific mission—to reach lost souls with the gospel of Jesus Christ and to motivate and train the rest of the soldiers in your platoon to do the same. Your squad sets the pace for an aggressive offensive into the kingdom of darkness on a search and rescue mission. ⬤

The battalion you serve in, the company you are a part of, the platoon you attend, and the squad you fight alongside are all connected through Christ. The challenging task of your squad is not only to rescue the lost but to motivate the rest of the army to invade by your side. As you set the pace for effective outreach, not only will your platoon be affected, but eventually your battalion, division, and someday, God willing, your entire army. That's called revival. That should be your ultimate goal as a squad. ⬤

Many squads of spiritual special forces have affected the entire world for God. From the "Haystack Revival" that sparked the modern day mission movement in America to the First and Second Great Awakenings, small groups of teens have been used by God to lead the way for revival for the last three hundred years. ⬤

THE E-TEAM STRATEGY . . . PRAYER–DARE–SHARE

Every field general worth his salt has a plan. General George S. Patton, the fiery leader of Third Battalion in World War II, once said, "A good plan violently executed now is better than a perfect plan next week."[1] ⬤

The Prayer–Dare–Share Strategy is a good plan. If you execute it with intensity and prayer, then God will use it to help you and your E-Team reach lots of lost teenagers from the context of your weekly youth group meeting. ✸

PRAYER

If you want to see your friends come to Jesus, start by praying. The apostle Paul wrote, "My heart's desire and prayer to God for the Israelites is that they may be saved" (Romans 10:1). Is your heart's desire and prayer to God for your friends, classmates, teammates, coworkers, family members, and neighbors that they may be saved from the power of sin and prison of Satan? ✸

Start a spiritual "hit list" of teens you will pray for every day to come to Jesus. As you pray for them, God will begin to open up the opportunities for you to share the good news of Jesus Christ with them so that their souls may be rescued from the powers of darkness. ✸

DARE

I remember getting the double-dare from friends growing up. Whether it was going up to that girl and asking her out or jumping off the cliff into the waters below, I almost always took the dare. When our friends dare us to do something, we tend to do it. Sometimes it gets us in trouble. But sometimes it saves a soul. This is the dare I want you to take: Will you dare your friends to come to youth group with you? ✸

When a friend invites you somewhere you go. Why? Because he or she is your friend. This is a tremendous opportunity to lead your friends to Jesus Christ. If they come to youth group with you and see the gospel in the excellence, feel the gospel in the acceptance, taste the gospel in the worship, and hear the gospel in your youth leader's talk, then it's going to be hard for them to say no to Jesus. ✹

The student evangelists who lead the most friends to Christ invite their friends to come to youth group every day. This is beyond inviting. This is stalking! And that's what I want to encourage you to do . . . stalk your friends for Jesus (OK, not literally, but you get the idea). Keep inviting your friends to come with you until they give up and give in. Once there, hopefully they will experience the love of God through the youth group you attend. Hopefully they will hear and see and feel and taste the gospel. Afterward you can share the gospel with them. ✹

SHARE

"What did you think of what my youth leader said?" ✹

All of a sudden you are in a nonthreatening conversation about spiritual things with your friend. This is a really easy time to bring up the gospel and engage your friend in a conversation about spiritual things. ✹

SHORT JUMP/LONG JOURNEY

For some of your friends it will be a short jump for them to come to Jesus. For others it will be a long journey. For those who are ripe and ready to believe it is a short jump. Sometimes they will trust Christ as their Savior right in the middle of the youth group meeting. For others it will be a long journey. It may take months or years for them to accept the claims of Christ. But don't give up. Walk with them each step of the way until they believe and receive. ✱

THE E-TEAM CONCEPT

An E-Team is a group of students within the youth ministry who lead the charge for evangelism in that youth ministry. It is comprised of teenagers who are passionate about reaching their friends for Jesus Christ. ✱

In a platoon of soldiers, there are different roles for different soldiers. There are those who provide leadership and training, those who handle communications, those who call in air support, and those who bandage the wounded. ✱

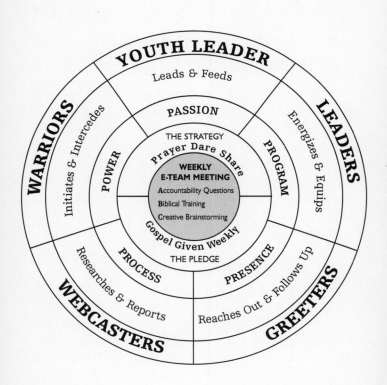

YOUTH LEADERS

The youth leader is the platoon leader who provides strategic leadership. Youth leaders lead and feed. They make sure that the youth meeting is done well and that the gospel is given clearly every week. ●

STUDENT LEADERS

Under the direction of the youth leader, student leaders energize and equip. They provide ongoing training for the rest of the teenagers in the youth group to share their faith and keep the entire youth group motivated to invite their friends using the Prayer–Dare–Share Strategy. These student leaders may also direct other outreach efforts, from collecting canned goods for a local shelter (and sharing the gospel with the people they encounter) to doing mall evangelism and short-term mission trips. ●

GREETERS

Like medics in the army, these warriors run to be at the side of newcomers. They make them feel comfortable, bandage wounds, answer questions, and generally make those who visit the youth group feel accepted. There is usually a squad of greeters who wait at the door or in the parking lot and welcome visiting students in, introduce them around, sit with them (and the friend who invited them), and walk them out when the whole thing is over. ●

The greeters also follow up new converts. Greeters follow up with the friend who invited the newcomer to see if the newcomer trusted in Jesus Christ as his or her

Savior. If the teen became a believer, then the greeter helps get him or her plugged in and growing in his or her newfound faith. ⊕

WEBCASTERS

These students are communication central. Using the Internet, these young warriors research and report. They provide online articles from Websites like www .dare2share.org, www.equip.org, www.apologeticsindex .org, www.impactapologetics.com, and lots of others that deal with subjects from "how to lead a Mormon to Christ" to "how you can help people grow in their faith." ⊕

Webcasters also communicate to the other students in the E-team, keeping them informed of the latest, greatest stories of students coming to Christ. If you launch an E-Team, Dare 2 Share Ministries is there to help you keep it going. Click on www.dare2share.org or www.eteam-revolution .net, fill out the webcaster report, and receive a free weekly e-zine called "Sustain and Maintain" packed full of useful outreach tools for you and your youth group. ⊕

PRAYER WARRIORS

Intercessors are the heart and soul of the E-Team. These prayer warriors lead the charge on their knees and provide "air support" for the rest of the group. They challenge all the students in the youth group to have a list of students that they are praying for every day to come to Christ. They launch special prayer initiatives where students pray and fast all night or are involved in a concert of prayer. ⊕

Without prayer the whole E-Team is simply another program. With prayer it is an unstoppable revolution. ⓑ

For free training curriculum and exciting updates on the revolution, check out the dare2share or e-team revolution Websites and learn more how to be a part of this powerful movement. ⓞ

JOIN THE REVOLUTION

Braveheart is the true story of William Wallace, a common man who amassed an army to fight against English tyranny. It is the story of one common man who united a nation by calling his fellow countrymen to launch a revolution and to win it. Launching it was easy— the Scottish had had their fill of English oppression and weren't going to take it anymore. More and more men rallied to Wallace's side, and they used guerilla tactics to assault the English army and overthrow English tyranny in tiny skirmishes. But the real test was yet to come. Again, to launch a revolution is easy . . . it takes common men and women with a compelling cause. But to win a revolution takes hardened warriors who are willing to lose everything to prevail. ⓞ

The real test came at the battle of Sterling where all the common men of Scotland gathered to face the full force of a formidable foe . . . the well-trained, well-financed army of England. ⓑ

One of my favorite scenes in one of my favorite movies is the first full-out battle between the English and the Scots. When the Scottish saw the glistening, intimidating armor of the English soldiers and heard the distant hoofbeats of the coming cavalry, this ragtag Scottish army was starting to leave the battlefront in paralyzing fear of the English. They were outmatched and vastly outnumbered. They were facing the challenge of defeating a near impossible foe, so many decided instead to leave and live. As the battle force was falling apart, in rode the unimpressed Wallace with his scarred crew of battle-hardened warriors. In the movie he addressed the crowd of scared soldiers with these unforgettable words,

Wallace: "I am William Wallace, and I see a whole army of my countrymen here in defiance of tyranny. You have come to fight as free men, and free men you are. What will you do without freedom? Will you fight?"

Soldier: "Against that? No, we will run, and we will live."

Wallace: "Aye, fight and you may die. Run and you'll live. At least awhile. And dying in your beds many years from now, would you be willing to trade all your days, from this day to that, to tell our enemies that they may take our lives, but they can never take our freedom!"

Wallace called them to go from launching a revolution to be willing to do what it takes to win the revolution. He called his men to count the cost and pay the price . . . and they did. ✿

William Wallace, in the end, counted the cost and paid the price. After his gruesome execution, the people of Scotland rebelled one last time under the leadership of Earl the Bruce. My second favorite scene in *Braveheart* is at the very end. There, gathered with his soldiers in a field of Banockberg, Earl the Bruce faced the opportunity to make a truce with England or charge ahead one last time in battle against the English. He turned to his soldiers and said, "You bled with Wallace . . . now bleed with me." Earl the Bruce then led them into one last battle, and they won their independence as a nation. ✹

The most powerful scene in the movie *Braveheart* is the execution of William Wallace. After finally being captured, the English decided to exact their revenge for years of violent attacks he had inflicted against them. As his tortures began, he was mocked by the onlooking crowd of English men and women. They applauded his every scream and moan. The sinister and evil religious leader who was appointed to oversee his torture mocked him every second along the way as well, asking Wallace to kiss the seal of England on his robe and pledge allegiance to the evil king of England. Wallace refused. ✹

The cheering crowd went wild with every new torture that was being inflicted upon Wallace. Finally, after all of the pain they could inflict, Wallace was strapped to a table where his clothes were cut off and he was disemboweled. The mocking crowd cringed at Wallace's pain, and shouts of "mercy" began to rise up from the throng of Englishmen. Then the religious leader leaned down to Wallace and whispered in his ear, "Just cry out the word 'mercy' and we will kill you quickly. Just say the word 'mercy' and you will cease from your pain." Choking through the pain Wallace tried to say something, and the hypocritical spiritual leader calmed the crowd and said, "The prisoner wishes to say a word." ✹

With the deafening silence of a quiet crowd Wallace, mustered all of his strength to draw air in his lungs, and with his last breath he screamed out the word "FREE-DOM!!!!!" ✹

He refused to give up. He refused to give in. He refused to give way until freedom was gained. As a result of his death Scotland won her independence. His courage in life and his bravery in death rallied a nation to fight and win. ✹

Like Wallace, the church in America is being assaulted. Our assault is by the Evil One himself. Strapping his prisoners to the rack by the chains of complacency and sin, Satan himself is torturing and taunting us until we scream out the word "mercy" and die. But I believe that the last breath in the lungs of the church in America today is you. It is going to take a new generation of Spirit-propelled, unstoppable teen evangelists who won't give up, give in, or give way until this nation and this world throw off the shackles of oppression and win the freedom that is in Christ Jesus. So what is the call? The call is to count the cost. The call is to die to self. The call is to win the revolution. The call is to just say one word with your last breath. That one word will rally the people of God . . . that one word will overthrow the evil of Satan . . . that one word will change a nation. With your last breath—with every breath—say "Jesus!" ✹

Revolution begins when you are willing to sacrifice everything for a cause. Your cause is Christ and the advancement of His kingdom. You are in the battle zone for the souls of your friends. You are in for the fight of their lives. ✹

PLATOON CHALLENGE

As a group talk about starting an E-Team.

1. Why do we or don't we need one as a youth group?

2. How could it look in the current youth ministry structure?

3. What would be our goals?

a. Number of students reached in the school year

b. Growth of the youth group

c. Percentage of new believers plugged into the youth group

d. Spiritual growth of our entire youth group

4. If we start one, when would be a good time to launch?

AN ARMY OF ONE

1. Write the name of one friend you will reach with the gospel within the next forty-eight hours:

_____

2. What changes do you need to make in your life before a movie could be made of your courage? Write three or four of them here:

NOTES

1: SOMEBODY HATES YOU

1. C. H. Spurgeon, *Spiritual Warfare in a Believer's Life* (Lynnwood, WA.: Emerald, 1993), 107.

5: SATAN'S HOME BOYS

1. Lewis Sperry Chafer, *Systematic Theology,* Volume 2 (Dallas: Dallas Seminary Press, 1947), 117.
2. C. S. Lewis, *The Screwtape Letters* (New York: Macmillan, 1982), 3.
3. Chafer, *Systematic Theology,* 121.
4. George Barna, *Third Millennium Teens* (Ventura, CA: Barna Research, 2000), 56–57.

6: TOUCHED BY AN ANGEL

1. Ron Rhodes, *Angels Among Us* (Eugene, OR: Harvest House, 1994), 61.
2. Augustus Hopkins Strong, *Systematic Theology: A Compendium* (Old Tappan, NJ: Revell, 1979), 445.
3. Lewis Sperry Chafer, *Systematic Theology,* Volume 2 (Dallas: Dallas Seminary Press, 1947), 17.
4. Rhodes, *Angels Among Us,* 99.

7: TEN MYTHS ABOUT SATAN AND SPIRITUAL WARFARE

1. Hank Hanegraaff, *The Covering* (Nashville: W Publishing Group, 2002), 12.
2. Richard Baxter, *The Reformed Pastor* (Portland, OR: Multnomah, 1982), 35–36.

8: HOW TO WIN THE WAR FOR THE SOULS OF YOUR FRIENDS

1. Richard Marcinko, *Leadership Secrets of the Rogue Warrior* (New York: Pocket Books, 1996), 10.
2. William A. Cohen, *Patton on Leadership: Strategic Lessons for Corporate Warfare* (Paramus, N.J.: Prentice Hall, 1999), 130.

MOODY
PUBLISHERS

THE NAME YOU CAN TRUST®